KU-033-427

Boomerang Joy

OTHER BOOKS BY BARBARA JOHNSON

Where Does a Mother Go to Resign?
Stick a Geranium in Your Hat and Be Happy!
Fresh Elastic for Stretched Out Moms
Pack Up Your Gloomees in a Great Big Box
Splashes of Joy in the Cesspools of Life
I'm So Glad You Told Me What I Didn't Wanna Hear
Mama, Get the Hammer! There's a Fly on Papa's Head!
Living Somewhere Between Estrogen and Death
The Joy Journal
Victory Is Mine

CO-AUTHOR ON

The Joyful Journey
We Brake for Joy!
Joy Breaks

BARBARA JOHNSON

Boomerang Joy

Joy that Goes Around, Comes Around

6 0   D E V O T I O N S

Illustrated by John McPherson

ZondervanPublishingHouse
Grand Rapids, Michigan

A Division of HarperCollinsPublishers

Requests for information should be addressed to:

ZondervanPublishingHouse
Grand Rapids, Michigan 49530

Library of Congress Cataloging-in-Publication Data

Johnson, Barbara (Barbara E.)
    Boomerang joy : joy that goes around, comes around / Barbara Johnson ; illustrated by John McPherson
      p. cm.
    ISBN: 0-310-22006-8 (hardcover : alk. paper)
    1. Women—Prayer-books and devotions—English. 2. Joy—Religious aspects—Christianity—Prayer-books and devotions—English. 3. Devotional calendars. I. Title.
BV4527.J618 1998
242'.643—DC21
                                        98-13817
                                          CIP

This edition printed on acid-free paper and meets the American National Standards Institute Z39.48 standard.

Interior design by Jody DeNeef
Cartoons by John McPherson

Printed in the United States of America

---

99 00 01 02 03 04 / ❖ DC/ 10 9 8 7 6 5 4 3 2 1

To my beloved endocrinologist,
Jeffrey S. Bodwin, M.D.,
who has encouraged me
in sharing the
boomerang principle
I lovingly dedicate this book

A SUNSHINE BOOMERANG

When a bit of sunshine hits ye,
After passing of a cloud,
When a bit of laughter gits ye
An' yer spine is feelin' proud,
Don't forgit to up and fling it
At a soul that's feelin' blue
For the minit that ye sling it
It's a boomerang to you!
      —CAPT. JACK CRAWFORD

CONTENTS

INTRODUCTION

Boomerang: a bent or angular throwing club typically flat on one side and rounded on the other so that it soars or curves in flight; esp: one designed to return near the thrower.

WEBSTER'S NINTH NEW COLLEGIATE DICTIONARY

Life: we're all in it together (some just deeper than others!). No matter how deep, we could all do with some boomerang skills. Used for war and hunting, boomerangs soar upward when missing a target, then curve in the air to return toward the thrower. They can be thrown more than one hundred yards before coming back; with skill, close enough to be caught by hand.

The game of life is a game of boomerangs. Our thoughts, deeds, and words return to us sooner or later with astonishing accuracy. If you're tired, worn by life, or just plain burned out, try throwing a little boomerang joy! Let's face it: there are times when your best friend is out of town, your husband out for the day, your pastor, counselor, and hairdresser out to lunch. You've got to hone your ability to fling a smile a mile. Sure as anything, it'll come back to you, more accurately each time you toss it out.

Let's honor the way of the aborigine, the originators of authentic boomerang power. Go hunting for humor. Use the tool that will soar away and curve into your own backyard. Fling it! Toss it! Sling it! Start right where you are. Get your throwing arm in shape by exercising the muscles on your funny bone. Get wacky, wild, and whimsical. Want happiness? Throw a little boomerang joy.

JOYFULLY,

Bart Johnson

TO THROW A BOOMERANG:

1. Grip with three fingers, curved side facing the body.
2. Use a stiff-arm, overhand delivery.
3. Flick the wrist just as boomerang leaves the hand to make it spin.

FLING OUT JESUS' JOY

*When the going gets tough—come on over . . .
and hide in the basement with me!*

No kidding! My life is full of complication and suspense. Not one of us knows what's going to happen next. Or how long we have to live. Or how long we have to love. That's why we have to make each moment count in a kind of boomerang way. Boomerang joy is the kind that smacks back to you when you add joy to someone else's life.

I want to tell you about something I have never before written or spoken of. And I'm telling about it not because I want to sound like Saint Barbara but because it is the best example of boomerang joy in my own life! Several years ago I began keeping a list of all the families Spatula Ministries had counseled in the previous twelve months, those who had lost children from AIDS, suicide, or in a few cases accidental death. When I first began, the list included only about 60 or 70 families. Last year it swelled to 370 families, largely because of the increase in AIDS.

I consider this project a birthday present to myself because I start every year on my birthday, December 14. I get

"WOW! THAT WAS *NEAT*, DAD! OK, TEACH ME HOW TO THROW IT! DAD?!"

up at four a.m. because of the three-hour time difference between the East and West Coasts and begin phoning each family who has lost a child during the year. Many of these parents are overwhelmed when I explain who I am and why I am calling. They're shocked that I remember them and surprised that anyone would care enough to make a long-distance call. You can hear the pleasure in their voices as they express their amazement.

I tell the parents that I know this will be their first Christmas without their child and that I understand their sorrow. There's usually a break in the conversation, and I can hear the sound of pent-up emotion. Crying. Voices laden with feeling, spilling out gratitude that someone remembered.

The time is unlimited on phone calls but let the parents express as much emotion as they can. Some haven't dared tell anyone why their son or daughter died, and I can hear the relief in their voices after we've talked. For many this is their first time opening up, draining the abscesses of pain in their hearts. We know that openness is to wholeness as secrets are to sickness, so we talk some more. Sometimes I pray with them, asking God to wrap them in His comfort blanket and be their healer during the holiday time. As we talk, I can actually hear their spirits lifting.

These calls are made every day until Christmas, and sometimes a couple days after. Then in the first few weeks of the new year, I receive an overwhelming flood of letters and cards from the folks I talked to. That is my boomerang joy! Parents tell me that the phone call was their best Christmas present—knowing that they were remembered, that they could actually speak their child's name and talk openly about their loss. That simple gesture made their Christmas bearable. A flow of joy comes back to me from all over the country.

At a convention recently in the Midwest, when closing my message, I felt compelled to explain a little button I wear that says, "Someone Jesus loves has AIDS." I pointed out to the crowd that it doesn't say, "Someone who loves Jesus" but "Someone Jesus loves." I want to make sure people understand that Jesus cares. That afternoon I couldn't help adding, "When we are brought into God's kingdom family, there are no abortions. Once we are sealed by His grace, we may fall into sin and lose our fellowship, but our relationship with God is still the same. We belong to God, and He will relentlessly love and pursue every prodigal." I had never addressed the issue as emphatically as I did that day.

After the meeting closed, two distraught young men appeared at my side. They were handsome guys in their late twenties, wearing tuxes because they were ushers at the arena. They had heard my concluding remarks, and confided that each had AIDS and that one of them had attempted suicide a few weeks earlier. Never before, they said, had they heard that God could love them. Instead they'd been told by Christians they were beyond redemption.

The fear and pain in the eyes of these young men melted as they began to realize not only that God loved them but that there was still time to get their hearts right with Him. As we said good-bye, they gave me the names and addresses of their mothers. No one knows how this story will end. At the end of this year I may find myself calling *their* parents with a message of comfort and hope. But whatever happens, I will not forget those two young men.

Who do you know that needs encouragement and a listening ear? Don't wait for their birthday to call. Pick up the phone and tell someone you care. As you spend yourself on others, you'll find yourself catching hold of a little boomerang joy!

UPLIFTER

He who refreshes others will himself be refreshed.
PROVERBS 11:25

WAY TO PRAY

Dear Lord, I love the way You were present with people, touching their wounds, allowing them to touch You, even the hem of Your garment. In Your presence is healing and joy. I realize I may be the only Jesus someone else may ever see. Help me express Your love when I don't know how to reach someone or what to say. Amen.

BOOMERANG PRACTICE

Why be normal? (Or as the title of Patsy Clairmont's book says, Normal Is Just a Setting on Your Dryer.)

I saw the words emblazoned on a bumper sticker attached upside down to a passing car: "Why be normal?" Yes! I thought. Why indeed? Where, I wondered, could I get a bumper sticker like that? But even if I had found one, I knew it wouldn't have looked nearly as provocative on my plain red Ford as it did on the lime green Citroën speeding by that day.

A few days later I read this: "I've always wanted to be normal; lately I've had a strong suspicion this is it." Some people wish they were normal, while others wish they weren't. I think I vacillate between those two desires. Mostly I have a hankering to be like everybody else—mentally adjusted, fairly happy, secure in the roles life has assigned me, and not too anxious about the future. I often wish to be normal but not dull.

But is everybody else really all that normal and well adjusted? No one knows better than I do that people hurt. As I travel across the country to various speaking engagements, I meet concealed hurt, disguised hurt, disjointed hurt. I bump up against surreal and denied hurt. Pain is a normal part of life.

That's why I say, Why be normal? Why not take as much joy as possible along the way so when hurt comes, we assimilate it better? Believe it or not, most people don't know how! When troubles come along in doses, many people complain and buckle under. I say we need emotional makeovers!

Getting an emotional makeover doesn't involve denying our problems to put on a happy face. It welcomes trials full-strength, all the time saying, "Come on, Lord, pour it on me! I know You love me. I accept every day as it comes, *filtered through Your love*. You know I can do this; You have confidence in me. In these troubles I take joy." Every day now I take joy—by refusing to be normal, by refusing to accept the lie that I have to feel miserable about the baggage, the stuff, the sickness, that trails me no matter how I try to hide or outwit it. I choose to do zany, kooky, and funny things to make myself and others laugh, like jumping on my trampoline to practice for the rapture!

And I fling joy—beyond my next-door neighbor's fence, clear across town, and into the universe. Then it curves right back to me. Sometimes with a whack on the head when I need it. Sometimes with a thwack into my heart. Sometimes landing with a crack at my feet. But it always comes back. No doubt about it.

"Whoops!" I yell. "Whoopee!" This is a game I can really get into. Someone said that's what it will be like in heaven when we throw our crowns at Jesus' feet. It will be a heavenly game of catch: He throws the crowns back to us and we throw them back to Him, all the while each of us elated by the other's glory and joy. If that's what heaven's like, I need a little boomerang practice now.

That's why I've decided to get into a good humor and stay that way. That's why I want to treat people with kindness and a smile wherever I meet them, regardless of how they treat me. The smile, the kindness, comes back. My boomerang joy commitment is not based on how I feel at any particular time. It's a habit I am cultivating to honor the way of the wild, the aborigine in me, the outback, the bird in the bush. After all, why be normal?

A newspaper columnist named Nancy Lambert says her idea for a self-help organization should be named TWITSS: The Whimsically Impaired Treatment Support Services. Try being a TWIT with me for a while. Let your joy out. One way I do that is to give people something to laugh about. How? I collect jokes and write down everything I hear that makes me brighten up. I make amusement a ministry because chuckles are better than a therapist. They are aloe vera for the sunburns of life. When the dumps take their toll, laughter provides the exact change to get you through.

Once, in my Spatula Ministries newsletter, I printed text from a greeting card that said, "Think of me as being your emotional bra." (You know, meaning I am an emotional support system for you.) But before long I received a letter saying that was "distasteful." I hear and understand what the writer wanted to say. That's OK. I've had my critics—those who want to keep me on the straight and narrow, restricting me to a slimmer kind of humor. They prune me and preen me. I don't mind, really; I just speed past and shout, "Why be normal?"

Whatever your troubles, try looking at them by the light of another source or a different star. Go ahead; don't be afraid. Find a wacky angle, a new twist. Don't offer trouble the energy you should be using to train your boomerang arm. Offer trouble a little serious thought, then turn it upside down and look at it through God-colored glasses. Chew on trouble's possibilities for making you smarter, better, stronger, kinder. Sample some weird and wonderful Jelly Bellies, Gobstoppers, or Sweet Tarts while you do that. Then take the curved weapon I call joy and toss trouble by its funny side out into the world.

Say, "God loves you; pass it along."

UPLIFTER

Ask and you will receive, and your joy will be complete.
JOHN 16:24

WAY TO PRAY

My Lord and Father, You are the God of all comfort, the God of all laughter, the God of all good humor that turns my churning world into a place where I can thrive. Even though I am not normal. Even when things are not OK. Even as I'm debated, dumped, or downsized. Thanks for being with me through it all and helping me rise above it all! Amen.

HOORAY FOR GARDENING!

Old florists never die; they just make other arrangements.

Old gardeners never die; they just spade away.

You can't go into a gift store these days without running smack into all kinds of gardening paraphernalia. It's in your face: Stepping-stones that say, "Wish," "Imagine," or "Wonder." Little signs that announce, "Garden angel" or "Mother's garden." Birdhouses of every description—a boarding home advertising, "Cheap cheap rent," Italian bird-restaurants, log cabin respites for ol' fisher birds, and many other creative habitations.

Gardening fever is upon us. It seems as though everyone is a gardener, even if they live in a big-city apartment. Even if they have eleven green thumbs. Even if they wouldn't pull weeds for a million dollars. Even if they don't know the difference between a spade and a rake. Even if they hate vegetables and bugs, are allergic to bees, or have spring allergies. Suddenly everyone is a gardening maniac. Even I perhaps one day will burst my buds of calm and blossom into full-blown hysteria—even gardening hysteria.

Are you like me? Well, there are certain things anybody can plant—sweet P's in a straight row, for instance: prayer, patience, peace, passion. But it's not enough for a gardener to love flowers. He or she also must hate weeds. As good plants grow, you pinch off bitter ones like panic, paranoia, and passivity. And by the way, while gardening, do squash pride. And please, lettuce love one another at all times.

We're all gardeners of the heart. Gardeners—because some ancient longing is built into us for the good, sweet earth. There is something evocative about the setting where Adam first met Eve. These two lovers walked with their Creator in the still of the evening as the Lord hit heaven's dimmer switch. There, at twilight, among the scent of roses and jasmine and apple blossoms, they savored a fellowship we can only dream about.

And wouldn't you love to have been in that garden outside Jerusalem two thousand years ago? The trees were budding, the flowers bursting through the ground. That morning as the sun was rising, Jesus wore His new body for the first time. In the hazy light of dawn He was mistaken for the gardener by a woman who had watched Him die. Surely she never forgot that wonderful encounter in the garden.

Begin now to cultivate your half acre of love. All it takes is a few seeds no larger than grains of sand. Jesus said if you have faith no bigger than the size of a mustard seed, "nothing will be impossible for you" (Matt. 17:20). Remember when you were a child, you could buy a little necklace with a single mustard seed in a tiny glass ball? I had one of those; how insignificant that seed looked. Today I meet people whose lives flower with the results of tiny deeds of goodness planted year after year. The rest of us harvest the fruit from their lives.

WHAT STARTED AS A HOBBY FOR CAROL
WAS SLOWLY BECOMING A FULL-SCALE
OBSESSION.

Often they haven't got a clue as to how God is using them. They weather storms and droughts and bugs and pestilence, just being faithful. They know that the blossom of a good deed fades with time but that the lasting perfume is the joy you receive from doing it.

The psalmist wrote, "Dwell in the land and enjoy safe pasture" (Ps. 37:3). A Chinese proverb says, "One who plants a garden plants happiness." An American proverb says, "One who plants a garden is not waiting around for someone else to bring her flowers." No, she is too busy picking bouquets to brighten the homes of everyone she loves!

If violets are God's apology for February, surely we can feed and groom and take a "start" of violet faith to everyone we know. Let the violet's deep blue color encourage you to keep believing, to wait for the promise of spring no matter how harsh the winter. Gardeners live by the signs of the seasons and know there is a time for everything, "a time to plant and a time to uproot" (Eccl. 3:2). They know there is a season for every color and taste. They know the brook would lose its song if God removed the rocks. They know rainbows promise enough rain and sunshine to grow everything in abundance.

Why the gardening mania? Why the books, calendars, accessories, decorations, tools, music, picture frames, furniture, clothes? Why are we so enchanted with white picket fences made into tables and chairs and headboards for the bed? Why the silk grapevines, sweet peas, and ficus trees for the bathroom, kitchen, and hall? Because we crave the sweet serenity of greens and golds and deep brown earth. Because fellowship with God began in a garden, and we long for that time and place. Because leaves quivering in the wind, blossoms nodding, grass ruffled by a breeze, remind us of our real home and the peaceful destiny awaiting us. Because when I cheer up with my geraniums, smile at my pansies, laugh with my petunias, they teach me about God's big greenhouse bursting with joy.

For now, I'll take seedlings on loan from heaven and share the growth. Mint in the pot on my back doorstep perks up afternoon tea; I'll invite a neighbor to share it. Bunches of parsley from the window box will flavor Aunt Sadie's stew. My pasta-loving daughter-in-love will relish fresh basil and rosemary. There are strawberries for Bill's breakfast, and rhubarb for Grandma's famous pie. We'll pick tomatoes for a just-out-of-the-earth salad to share with everyone on the block.

Gardening burns calories, lowers risk of heart attack, slows soil erosion, and provides shelter for a host of microlife. So hooray for gardening! Get your gloves muddy, your face tanned, and your knees crinkled here on earth. Nurture faith and love. Keep believing in the harvest. God will make something beautiful out of your effort and energy.

The most beautiful gardens bloom in the heart!

UPLIFTER

Now the LORD God had planted a garden . . .
GENESIS 2:8

WAY TO PRAY

Dear heavenly Father, thank You for making me a gardener of spirit. Help me sow kindness and reap blessing to heap into the lives of others. Amen.

A STANDING OVATION

WOW is MOM turned upside down.

When I first began speaking for groups and church engagements, Spatula Ministries had just begun. We called it Spatula because so many hurting parents feel they have to be scraped off the ceiling after discovering their child is gay. The first time I was invited to share my story, it was at a women's banquet in a town about an hour's drive from home. They asked how much I charged to speak, but I just told them that a tank of gas for my car would suffice; it was a compliment just to be invited.

Arriving at the banquet, I walked in, delighted at the decorations. Spatulas were hung all over the room and dangled from a large banner that said, "BARBARA JOHNSON WOW!" Each centerpiece said the same thing. The words were even emblazoned on the podium and hanging in front of the platform. Wow! I could hardly believe it. It was my first speaking engagement, and these ladies were already sold on me. What a welcome!

While I was seated, waiting to be introduced, a woman stepped to the mike and began: "We, the women of WOW, . . ." Uh-oh! Could WOW actually be the name of this group? How could I have taken it personally? Being a speaker was so new to me, and I had grabbed the tribute to myself. Glancing at my program, I realized that WOW referred not to Barbara Johnson but to Women of the Word.

I composed myself and rose to the podium, my own weakness and vulnerability fresh in my mind. Any gifts I had were given to me by God. With these ladies I was just another MOM who wanted to do the right thing. I was as ordinary as the most plain mother in the room. But I was also as extraordinary as each of them. For in God's eyes each one of us is WOW! Each of these ladies was as WOW as the most glamorous speaker or spiritual mentor in the country. That day I found myself among one hundred of the most amazing women I've ever been with, before or since.

Under the blood of Jesus and in the kingdom of heaven, we are all WOW! and Amen! As colaborers, we are to esteem each other highly—in love—for the sake of the work (1 Thess. 5:12). What characters there are in a gathering of women. What depth, wisdom, and motivation I meet as I travel. The next time you are in a place with Christians, don't just wait passively for the program to start or the sermon to begin. Look around you. On every side is incredible talent, emotion, and compassion in your fellow believers. Pick out one or two women you would like to meet. Afterward find out who they are and what they care about. How do they invest themselves in the world, their families, their friends? Give them a squeeze. Encourage them. Say "WOW!" to another woman who is working her heart out, trying to do the right thing in spite of obstacles, setbacks, and miscommunication.

I heard a story about a mother of four teenage daughters, about the same size as she. To keep her own laundry from disappearing into their drawers by mistake, this mother started marking her underwear "MOM." Finding her dresser drawer empty one morning, she went straight to the girls. "Do any of you have underwear that says 'MOM' on it?" she asked. One daughter spoke up quickly. "No, all of mine say 'WOW'!"

Everybody has a story. It may not be as cute as this one, and it may never be written down. Not everyone will be called upon to tell their story; not everyone will want to. But we can seek out the scared, the shy, the sad, and give them a transfusion of faith so they can go on living their story with courage. There is some area in each woman's life where she deserves a standing ovation. Let's be quick to applaud each other.

Anthropologists studying the clapping behavior of infants believe that applause at the end of a pleasing performance may be instinctive. At conferences and conventions, I've noticed that many speakers are unprepared to receive a standing ovation. Some raise their hands as if to offer the glory to God. Others keep bowing like the peasant lady in *The Sound of Music*. I always wondered what I would do if it happened to me. Then one of my friends told me, "Just walk up to the mike and start singing, 'He is Lord. He is Lord …' Shift the focus to heaven, where it belongs."

In being moms and wives and friends, our most pleasing performances of life, we recognize that we are really a small piece of God's big puzzle. It takes each of us working together, worshiping together, giving everything we have. The crowning achievement is when we see it all come together. Everyone is in her own place, shining, so the whole kingdom shines.

WOW!

UPLIFTER

In humility consider others better than yourselves.

PHILIPPIANS 2:3

WAY TO PRAY

Thank You, Lord, for making me a conduit of Your love. I don't have to shrivel or shrink. I pray that through me others will see Your glory made real. Amen.

GOD'S KINGDOM FIREWORKS

~℮

Enthusiasm, like the flu, is contagious—
we get it from one another.

For eighteen years our support group for parents of homosexuals has met monthly in a church across from Disneyland. Strangely enough, many of our members' children worked at Disneyland as those life-sized characters who walk around in costumes, signing autographs and getting photographed with tourists. Last month our group was talking about this, and a new member, who'd been quiet the whole meeting, finally admitted she was Mom to a well-known character at another Los Angeles attraction. She'd been embarrassed to admit it until she heard everyone else's stories.

During the summer months our meetings are always interrupted by the 9:30 p.m. fireworks over Disneyland. For years it's been this way. Just when we're getting around to prayer, the exploding bangs and booms and rumbles start. I always thought, *Oh, my goodness, those fireworks; now we have to listen to that again!* I'd usually get irritated and annoyed—until one evening a couple from Iowa joined us. As soon as the fireworks started, they sat up, eyes twinkling. "Oh, the fire-

THE DOWNSIDE OF GROWING UP A
BLOCK AWAY FROM DISNEYLAND.

works!" they exclaimed. There was wonder in their faces. They were excited and suddenly animated. "Can we stop for a few minutes to watch them?" they asked. "Imagine! Disneyland right across the street!"

The rest of us looked at each other and blinked. We had always simply "put up" with the noise. Suddenly, in our midst were two people helping us see it from a different perspective. To them the fireworks were not a problem but a possibility. Instead of feeling annoyed, they felt delighted!

Nothing has been the same since that couple from Iowa sat among us with their simple joy. Now when 9:30 rolls around, we no longer look at our watches and groan. Instead we look up with light in our faces, into each others eyes, and say, "Oh, the fireworks!" It's a reminder not to take our problems so heavy-heartedly, a reminder to think of the possibilities within each problem and to know there is light even in the darkest sky.

Have you ever thought about how to recapture that precious sense of wonder?

Try this: Think of everything you normally take for granted. Make a list of the most ordinary, tedious things that happen every day over and over in your life. Now imagine a homeless man or woman coming to live with you for a day, sleeping in your guest room, showering in your bathroom, eating what you eat, going where you go. How do you think they would feel about this one day in a real house in a real neighborhood with a real family? What do you think they would say about the line of soaps and lotions in your bathroom cupboard? The ointments and medicines in your medicine chest? The linens and soft blankets? The furnace that blows heat through the floor?

Or imagine you died, then were miraculously brought back to live one more week on earth. What would you say?

Who would you see? Where would you go? Experts say people who narrowly escape death look at things in a way the rest of us never will. Everything looks different, more vibrant.

"Oh, the fireworks!" The magic kingdom, the marvelous kingdom of our God, is right across the street regardless of where we live. When the parents of Disney characters come to our meetings, we give thanks and remember that Jesus loves their talented kids. After all, we are all characters out of God's great big book of tales, with our own gifts and eccentricities. We may as well get enthused and infect everyone we meet with His amazing love and power. Let the fireworks begin!

UPLIFTER

They recognized him ... and they were filled with wonder and amazement.

ACTS 3:10

WAY TO PRAY

Dear almighty God and Father, You have filled my life with exactly the right people and the right scene for me. I want to see the possibilities in all the seeming tragedies that make up my life. How interesting would a story be if there were no obstacles to overcome? I'm thankful You let me know difficulty and yet promised to be with me in it. Thank You for what this is going to bring out in my character and my faith. No matter what, I don't want to miss Your fireworks—especially the ones happening in my own backyard. Amen.

NESTLE, DON'T WRESTLE

*Most of us will miss out on life's big prizes: the Pulitzers,
the Heismans, the Oscars. But we're all eligible for
a pat on the back, a kiss on the cheek, a thumbs-up sign!*

Last year I watched Billy Graham being interviewed by
Oprah Winfrey on television. Oprah told him that in her
childhood home, she used to watch him preach on a little black-
and-white TV while sitting on a linoleum floor. She went on to
tell viewers that in his lifetime Billy has preached to twenty million people around the world, not to mention the countless
numbers who have heard him whenever his crusades are broadcast. When she asked if he got nervous before facing a crowd,
Billy replied humbly, "No, I don't get nervous before crowds,
but I did today before I was going to meet with you."

Oprah's show is broadcast to twenty million people
every day.

She is comfortable with famous stars and celebrities but
seemed in awe of Dr. Billy Graham. When the interview
ended, she told the audience, "You don't often see this on my
show, but we're going to pray." Then she asked Billy to close

in prayer. The camera panned the studio audience as they bowed their heads and closed their eyes just like in one of his crusades. Oprah sang the first line from the song that is his hallmark—"Just as I am, without a plea . . ."—misreading the line and singing off-key. But her voice was full of emotion and almost cracked.

When Billy stood up after the show, instead of hugging her guest, Oprah's usual custom, she went over and just nestled against him. Billy wrapped his arm around her and pulled her under his shoulder. She stood in his fatherly embrace with a look of sheer contentment.

I once read the book *Nestle, Don't Wrestle* (by Corrie ten Boom). The power of nestling was evident on the TV screen that day. Billy Graham was not the least condemning, distant, or hesitant to embrace a public personality who may not fit the evangelical mold. His grace and courage are sometimes stunning.

In an interview with Hugh Downs on the *20/20* program, the subject turned to homosexuality. Hugh looked directly at Billy and said, "If you had a homosexual child, would you love him?"

Billy didn't miss a beat. He replied with sincerity and gentleness, "Why, I would love that one even more."

When I related that comment to an audience of ten thousand people, they stood and applauded his words. The simplicity of his statement transcends our pettiness, heartbreak, and lack of clarity on an issue that polarizes and frustrates the nation and the church. The title of Billy's autobiography, *Just As I Am*, says it all. His life goes before him, speaking as eloquently as that charming southern drawl for which he is known.

If, when I am eighty years old, my autobiography were to be titled *Just As I Am,* I wonder how I would live now? Do

I have the courage to be me? I'll never be a Billy Graham, the elegant man who draws people to the Lord through a simple one-point message. But I hope to be a woman who is real and compassionate and who might draw people to nestle within God's embrace.

Any one of us can do that. We may never win any great awards or be named best dressed, most beautiful, most popular, or most revered. But each of us has an arm with which to hold another person. Each of us can pull another shoulder under ours. Each of us can invite someone in need to nestle next to our heart.

We can give a pat on the back, a simple compliment, a kiss on the cheek, a thumbs-up sign. We can smile at a stranger, say hello when it's least expected, send a card of congratulations, take flowers to a sick neighbor, make a casserole for a new mother. Do you know how to give a high five? Say "I love you" in language your teenager will understand? Back off even when you have a right to take the offensive?

Do you make it a point to speak to a person who shows up alone at church? Buy a hamburger for a homeless man? Call your mother on Sunday afternoons? How about picking daisies with a little girl? Or taking a fatherless boy to a baseball game? Did anyone ever tell you how beautiful you look when you're looking for what's beautiful in someone else?

Billy complimented Oprah when asked what he was most thankful for; he said, "Salvation given to us in Jesus Christ," then added, "and the way you have made people all over this country aware of the power of being grateful."

When asked his secret of love, being married fifty-four years to the same person, he said, "Ruth and I are happily incompatible."

How unexpected. We would all live more comfortably with everybody around us if we would find the strength in being grateful and happily incompatible. Let's take the things that set us apart, that make us different, that cause us to disagree, and make them an occasion to compliment each other and be thankful for each other. Let us be big enough to be smaller than our neighbor, spouse, friends, and strangers. Every day. Nestle, don't wrestle.

UPLIFTER

Offer your bodies as living sacrifices, holy and pleasing to God—this is your spiritual act of worship.

ROMANS 12:1

WAY TO PRAY

Almighty God and Father, how wonderful that You created us so differently yet each precious in Your sight. Each one of us is the apple of Your eye. Help me to be aware that the people You've put into my life are treasures. I pray for their salvation and well-being. Thank You for choosing me to love other people into Your kingdom. Amen.

THE GENIUS OF KIDS

*Art Linkletter to little girl: "What do you think
we're supposed to learn from the Bible story where
Jesus turned water into wine at the wedding?"*

*Little girl to Art Linkletter: "We learn that
the more wine we have, the better the wedding!"*

My husband and I recently watched a TV special that paid
tribute to Art Linkletter's years producing *Kids Say the
Darndest Things,* which was devoted to making kids and their
conversations special. Bill Cosby was the host, and he began
the program by showing fifteen hilarious video clips from
Linkletter's original show. After each clip an individual was
introduced—the same child all grown up, to greet Linkletter
with a big hug! Was Art Linkletter surprised!

But that was the least of it. At the end of the program,
Cosby announced that the studio audience was filled with
folks who, as kids, had appeared on Linkletter's show. About
four hundred people stood, holding children of their own or
with their entire families! They were introduced to Linkletter
as his face lit up with joy and amazement. He was overwhelmed with teary-eyed surprise. This man spent much of

his life and talent infusing others with joy, especially children. Now the program managers had tracked down the kids he had interviewed from all over the country—to bring *him* joy. What a boomerang effect this had! Here was a man who enchanted us by looking at things from a child's point of view. Now grown-up kids trekked across the stage to greet him with huge smiles and embraces.

Kids are people who seem to pay as little attention to discouragement as possible. They catch a ray of sunshine and hold on tight. They are masters at the best kind of assertiveness—barging right into life. Kids know that a good laugh and a long sleep are the best cures for what ails you—and that you should never buy a coffee table you can't put your feet on.

If kids could tell parents the secret to raising them right, they'd say, "Spend half as much money and twice as much time on us!" They'd say, "Tickle and touch us more. Play with us, and then you can teach us anything you want." They'd say, "We're listening to everything you *don't* say. We're watching everything you do."

I heard about a little girl who lost her hair during chemotherapy treatments. When she came home from the hospital, her mother and father had shaved their heads to celebrate the occasion. I read about a boy who also lost his hair to chemotherapy, and all the boys in his class welcomed him back to school by shaving their heads, too. This kind of object lesson speaks volumes to kids. Hard lessons and brilliant sacrifices say "I love you" more forcefully than all the toys or gadgets or treats in the world.

In *How to Win Grins and Influence Little People* (Honor Books) Clint Kelly gives parents great ideas. Here are a few.

- Grab your child in a bear hug and say, "You are a living miracle!"
- Ask your child to laugh for you, then say, "I love that sound. It makes me want to laugh, too."
- Leave a note on the bathroom mirror: "Good morning, Brenda. What a fine smile you have!"
- Record your child's laughter and play it back once in a while. Say, "Now that's music to my ears!"
- Say, "You're so much fun to be with. Let's play!"

As a parent, you recognize your child's vulnerability. Knowing you could easily use it against them, you choose not to. Instead you find a way to honor their weakness and hallow their childish innocence. You fly the flag of joy from the castle of their life every day they live under your roof. You get down on their level and make sure you're having as good a time as they are.

Nothing is as precious as the giggles shared with a child. It's like the tinkling of a silver bell. Sometimes it's like a foghorn. But if your kids don't make you laugh, you're missing out on one of the biggest mother lodes in history. Maybe you need to loosen your collar and kick off your shoes. Take off anything constricting and uncomfortable. Pull out your bows and combs and rubber bands and mess up your hair. Risk a broken nail or two.

Why not try a few of these suggestions to become a child again?

"I USED TO GET ALL BENT OUT OF SHAPE WHEN THE KIDS STAINED SOMETHING, UNTIL I GOT A BRAINSTORM AND TURNED THEIR STAINS INTO A MEMORIAL TOUR."

- Go to a local park and feed the geese out of your hand.
- Don't forget to take your toys into the bath with you, bubbles 'n all.
- Congratulate yourself on a job well done, with a gold star.
- Carry a bright, canary yellow umbrella on rainy days.
- Drink hot chocolate with marshmallows and whipped cream.
- Pray with the heartfelt sincerity of a child.
- Laugh and giggle often.

I found that time just went too fast with my sons. Before I knew it, two of them were gone. Before I knew it, there was not another chance to have a Jell-O fight in the kitchen, throw a few baseballs, or laugh ourselves silly over a prank. Martin Luther said, "If you can't laugh in heaven, then I don't want to go there." I'm looking forward to an eternity of laughing with my boys on the other side of the pearly gates. I hope the two waiting for me there are cooking up some crazy pranks to play on one another.

Keep happiness very close to the surface of your life. If you're going through deep waters, financial trouble, serious stress at work, double deadlines, bitter blowouts with a spouse, it's even more important that you make yourself available to your kids—not just for their sake but for yours. *You* need them. Don't pull away because you think you're no fun right now. You need their ability to hope and to be happy.

Did you know researchers say that the simple act of turning your lips up (instead of down) stimulates good feelings? No matter how down you feel, how rotten, try smiling at yourself in every mirror you pass. First thing in the morning. Last thing at night. Broaden those luscious lips. Twist them toward heaven. You'll feel perkier faster if you smile than you would if you wallowed in gloomy thoughts. (Think of what your grandma used to say: "Imagine your face frozen into a frown!")

Then remember to *ask* your kids more than you *tell* them. Formulate a few prize-winning questions inspired by Art Linkletter, Bill Cosby, or Bill Nye the Science Guy. Resolve to find out what your child is feeling or thinking, with no preconceived notions of a right or wrong answer. Ask what she would invent if given all the money in the world to develop it. Ask her about her wildest dreams. Ask her what she would be if she were a color, a wild animal, a member of the circus. Where would she go if she were a great adventurer?

Magic moments don't require special circumstances. You can tickle your kid when you tuck her into bed. You can kiss her toes and the tips of every finger. You can ask about her dearest wish when you're stirring the spaghetti or putting together a sack lunch. You find her soft spots easier when she's very glad or very sad. Tap into who she is at those times when she's not busy proving herself to you and everybody else.

Every time your child sees you happy and investing in her emotionally, you're binding her closer with invisible rope. If the rope starts to unravel, tie a knot in the end and hang on! Kids are like bouncing balls—they'll always take you by surprise. At least I hope they will. That's the way it's supposed to be. That's the way you maximize the joy.

Stay in the game. Don't ever give up. Twelve hugs a day—that's the minimum—don't have to be administered the same way twice. Keep up the attention. Let them know how cute you think they are. How smart! How witty! Let them know how much fun you think they are. Lay your head in her lap once in a while and listen. If she is not in a mood to talk, listen to her heart beat or stomach gurgle; if you can get close enough, listen to what she is thinking. Kids say the darndest things—in the most amazing ways.

To be in your child's memories tomorrow, you have to be in their lives today!

UPLIFTER

Whoever welcomes a little child like this in my name welcomes me.
MATTHEW 18:5

WAY TO PRAY

Dear Lord, how great it is, the way You made children the treasures they are. I applaud Your creativity! Your sense of humor! Your love for life and humans like me! Thank You for the kids You have put in my life. I commit to receive the youngest, most insignificant, as I would receive You, were You to visit me. I love You Lord; give me grace to love little ones—and learn from them—the same way. Amen.

"MARGE? I'M AFRAID WE'VE GOT TO
CANCEL FOR DINNER TONIGHT. ED'S
COME DOWN WITH SWINE FLU."

UNQUENCHABLE GRINS

Girl Receives Pig-Heart Transplant;
Now She Can't Stay Out of the Mud

ACTUAL HEADLINE, *WEEKLY WORLD NEWS*

I spotted this headline as I was standing in line at the grocery checkout. Who makes these things up, anyway? What a blast it would be to work at that paper and come up with one bizarre headline after another. Their staff must have hilarious brainstorming sessions! And who buys this tabloid, anyway?

Some say truth is stranger than fiction; others say it isn't stranger, just more rare. One thing is sure: if you tell the truth, there's less to remember! Seriously, think of all the weird things that have ever happened to you and the people you know. If you've been through difficulties, as I have, try writing them into *Weekly World News* headlines like "Local Mom Goes Bald When Daughter Dates Space Alien." Go ahead, amuse yourself!

Then think about your life in politically correct terms: Do you know how you can tell if you're codependent? When you die, you see someone else's life pass before your eyes!

No matter what, don't ever let yesterday use up too much of today. If it sneaks up on you, turn the tables on it.

Like interest rates, make trouble work *for* you, not *against* you. You don't always need a comedian to make you laugh. Once you get started, you can pull a few one-liners out of the bag yourself. When someone says, "Life is hard," say, "I prefer it to the alternative, don't you?" When somebody else complains about getting old, answer, "Right now, I'm just sitting here being thankful that wrinkles don't hurt!"

Life is too short to spend it being angry, bored, or dull. That was never God's intention. Maybe boredom and dullness aren't on any list of sins in the Bible, but they will sap your joy if you tolerate them.

Don't swallow Satan's lie that you have to keep swallowing bitter pills all your life. Fight back by developing and relishing a divine sense of humor, the gift God builds into your personality.

Got a problem? Make it an occasion to laugh. Live in a small town where everybody knows your business? Look at it this way: even when you don't know what you're doing, someone else does. Concerned that your teenagers are never home? Try creating a pleasant and inviting atmosphere—and then let the air out of their tires. Worried about not being able to keep up with everything and everyone? Recognize once and for all that you're over the hill when you start spelling relief N-A-P.

No matter how old they grow, some people never lose their beauty. They merely move it from their faces into their hearts. According to psychologists, the happiest age is fifty. Perhaps by then we've learned to accept the fact that life is weird and things simply turn out as they turn out. No use sweating it. God uses all kinds of circumstances to tweak our lives. By age fifty we've pretty much decided that the second half of our life is going to be better than the first, because we like ourselves exactly as we are. Now that early baby boomers are turning fifty, surely there's a happier world on the horizon. Get ready to rock!

No matter how old you are, belonging to Jesus Christ means you've been given a heart transplant. With a new heart, He gives the power to be joyful, exuberant, and thankful. Eternal values replace temporary ones. He forgives our sins and rehabilitates our past. As a new creation in Christ, don't make the mistake of ruining the present by blaming yourself for past mistakes. God is a gentle heavenly eraser. He erases slowly sometimes but leaves no trace and doesn't tear the paper.

Our rebirth takes us to places we never dared to imagine. Regeneration catapults us to achieve things we never thought possible: to rejoice in suffering, be patient in adversity, love our enemies, do good to those who do us wrong.

We are going to inherit the new heaven and the new earth. If we could see now all God has planned for us, we'd be beside ourselves with anticipation and joy. We'd be going around with an unquenchable grin on our faces and a boisterous song in our hearts. Not deceived by pain, we'd be absolutely certain of our future. Our lives would inspire exciting headlines rather than dull platitudes.

To be in Christ is to live a life that is anything but a cliché. Watch out! God is making you authentic. Real. Rubbing off your fake fur. Changing your outlook. Giving you new desires. Making you marvelous. Fulfilling what you were created for. He is making you the "Queen of Quite a Lot," enlightening you for kingdom work.

Open your arms wide to God's imagination at work in you. Be brave. Then braver still. Never resist His insistence on your perfection. He is working all things together for good, not just for you and yours but for people you've never met and may not meet until your paths cross in heaven.

So go ahead and imagine the way-out headlines your life may inspire in heaven. Envision your name in lights on the marquee of paradise. Then live it to the full. Get close to God and watch what happens!

UPLIFTER

You hem me in—behind and before; you have laid your hand upon me. Such knowledge is too wonderful for me, too lofty for me to attain.
PSALM 139:5–6

WAY TO PRAY

Father God, You know everything about me. Everything I'm thinking. Every detail of my day. You are changing me. Loving me. Leading me. No matter how boring my life gets, I'm in it for the long haul. I'm sticking with You, come what may. Amen.

NEVER OUTGROW MOTHERHOOD

Kids are like sponges—they absorb all your strength and leave you limp, but give 'em a squeeze and you get it all back!

Every day is a happy-Mother's-Day for the children of moms who are elastic, who can stretch. Who but a mother puts up with cranky toddlers or irritable teenagers free of charge? Who else gets up to make her own breakfast on her birthday? Who changes the empty toilet paper rolls? Never tires of inquiring, "Did you flush?" Lies awake on Saturday nights listening for the last chick to return to the nest? Who gathers all her eggs, puts them all in one basket, and then gives it to God?

One day a mother was baring her heart to a friend, telling of a daughter gone astray. "If she were my daughter," replied the friend, "I would kick her out."

The mother thought for a moment, then said, "Yes, if she were your daughter, so would I. But she's mine, and I can't do that." That is how moms are.

Of course, we moms never live up to all the sentimental stuff said about us. We all have bad days. (You know you're having one, by the way, when you gently tuck the dirty

"LET'S SEE NOW, HELEN. YOU'RE HERE
FOR WHAT? A TUMMY TUCK? NO,
HERE IT IS. A FACE-LIFT!"

clothes into bed and stuff the kids into the hamper!) The truth is that by the time you learn everything you need to know to be a mom, you're unemployed. But don't sweat it. Eventually you get to become a grandma, carrying pictures where your money used to be.

Be glad you have a stretchy, sticky mother's heart. Loving kids is not just about the kids. Raising one or two teaches you to manage crises and carry heavy loads in one arm while reaching out to someone else with the other. Pretty soon, walking the extra mile will be no biggie. Mopping up spills in other people's lives will become second nature. Let's face it: after raising two or three children, what could possibly "gross you out" anymore? (That reminds me of the mom who said, "I love to give homemade gifts; which one of my kids would you like?")

Every family tree, after all, has a little sap. Mothers get sentimentalized in pictures, books, and stories merely because they seem to glide effortlessly through any kind of upheaval. But it only *appears* effortless; really we're numb.

- We hang on so tight to hope—any last shed of it—that our fingers get callused; the soreness disappears.
- We know how to get out of tangles, because our children pull us into so many of them.
- We know how to mend a wounded heart, because ours has been broken several times.
- We know that the real art of raising kids is not only to say the right thing at the right time but to leave unsaid the wrong thing at the most tempting moment.

No, moms are not immortalized in literature and art because we are glorious creatures inherently good. The truth is, we've been knocked down and muddied more times than we care to remember. But we didn't stay down. Our love is tough and tender; if it weren't, we wouldn't be here now. Poets pay tribute to us precisely because our job is so tough. And that's what makes it so rewarding.

A wise man said that mothers are like Moses—"They never get to enter the Promised Land. Instead they lead others to a world they will not see." Let's face it: we can lead our kids to the borders of the Promised Land, but they have to go in and take the territory on their own. Worrying about them is like sitting in a rocking chair—it gives you something to do, but it doesn't get you anywhere. The years we have to shape their character are not many, but they are potent. The little moments—weighed together—impact everything our children will become. *Our* caresses become the way they treat others, *our* face the mirror reflecting their own, *our* arms the anchor that holds fast during their storms. Never mind the little boy who prayed, "Father, forgive us our trespasses, as we *give* it to those who trespass against us"; enjoy your children and teach them while they are still on your side!

Henry Ward Beecher wrote, "When God thought of mothers, He must have laughed . . . ." We might as well laugh, too, dazed by how much there is to teach and how fast the time flies. Let's laugh at the ketchup on the walls and the smudges on the furniture. At the bats and balls and broken windows. At the goofy clothes in preadolescence and the lurches and lunges into independence later on. And let's not forget to laugh at ourselves. And keep laughing. Dance with joy and keep dancing.

You never know how God is working through your prayers or how He is using what you try to do, even when you don't see results. Live motherhood to the hilt. Bequeath your kisses and your discipline generously. Raise the standard of faith along with a finger to scold or correct. Spread your arms wide to a kid with a skinned knee. Lift a chin, hold a hand, tickle a foot. Keep the good times glowing. Make sure praise is flowing. You are a mother. Be glad!

UPLIFTER

But his mother treasured all these things in her heart. And Jesus grew in wisdom and stature, and in favor with God and men.
LUKE 2:51–52

WAY TO PRAY

Dear God, You know I feel so easily let down by my children, and sometimes I know I let them down. But they are treasures. I pray Your will be done in their lives despite my failures or theirs. I want them to love You. Please hold them close. (Me too, Lord.) Amen.

"WE FELT SOMETHING ROLL INTO OUR FEET AND WHEN WE BENT DOWN WE FOUND THESE."

WHATEVER, LORD!

*Part of learning "Whatever, Lord!" is accepting
the fact that there is a God, and I am not He.*

I was flying from Minneapolis to California, or so I thought,
when the pilot announced we were returning to our port of
departure. "Whatever for?" we all wondered, groaning and
complaining. We were already three hours into the trip. The
pilot explained that the aircraft couldn't get enough altitude
to clear the Rocky Mountains near Denver. It sounded pre-
posterous, since the flight routinely traveled west via Denver
without a hitch. Despite our mutterings, we turned around
and headed back to Minneapolis.

Once on the ground, I called my sister, who had taken me
to the airport several hours earlier. She asked, "Where are you?"

"Back in Minneapolis," I surprised her.

"You should be in California by now! What happened?"

It wasn't long before the airplane mechanics found the
problem. One of them had left a vacuum hose in the door, pre-
venting the seal from being tight enough to allow the cabin to
be pressurized and thus enable the plane to clear the Rockies.

A simple error by a careless mechanic drained the airplane's power to soar. As a result, over one hundred passengers

had to go back to first base, unable to clear the obstacles in their path. Amazing what will keep us grounded, isn't it?

How like our daily lives, I thought, trying my best to laugh. I couldn't help but think of all the things that prevent me from soaring in the kingdom of God. What drains me of the Holy Spirit? What kind of vacuum hose saps me of strength and resilience? OK, here's my list (you can make your own).

Failure to live with intention
Failure to love with abandon
Failure to practice prayer
Failure to walk to the edge of my faith
Failure to take one step more

I don't know about you, but I want to do more than survive life. It's not enough to just flap my wings a little before I hit the ground and get plowed under. I want to mount up like the eagle and glide over rocky crags, nest in the tallest of trees, dive for nourishment in the deepest of mountain lakes, and soar on the wings of the wind. I want to live at high altitudes, close to the Almighty. I want to try new things and sail over obstacles that loom on the horizon.

But there are challenges. I live with a medical condition that requires special effort to practice wellness. I am a wife and mother, mother-in-law, and grandmother. I travel frequently. I have to meet publishing deadlines. I am in my so-called soaring sixties, right up there with gals like Shirley Temple and Minnie Mouse! My life is full of high speeds and wild swings. I often need studied judgment on when to say yes and when to say no. It's so easy to let busyness bog me down.

I challenge you: What's your personal vacuum hose that keeps you from soaring? Go to the source. Think about what you can change. Pray for illumination. Let go of worry. Follow the disciplines outlined in the Bible. Communicate with the Pilot as well as the ground crew. You may have to retrace some steps to get it right. But it's worth it. Better than crashing and burning.

Live every day to fulfill your personal mission. God has a reason for whatever season you are living through right now. A season of loss or blessing? A season of activity or hibernation? A season of growth or incubation? You may think you're on a detour, but God knows the best way for you to reach your destination.

Get ready to take off. Climb. Ascend. Soar. Do whatever is necessary to remove the hoses that drain your energy or force you backward. When you do go backward, ease up, appreciate your fellow passengers, and take it all in stride, then get going again. Don't give up and take the bus. It's better to fly. Remember that whatever happens, you are not alone way up there, for "underneath are the everlasting arms" (Deut. 33:27).

UPLIFTER

Praise the LORD, O my soul, and forget not all his benefits—who forgives . . . heals . . . redeems . . . crowns . . . satisfies . . . so that your youth is renewed like the eagle's.

PSALM 103:2–5

WAY TO PRAY

My heavenly Father, I want to use the few years You've given me to take flight in Your kingdom. I'm going to live today as if it were the only day I had to live for You. Bless other people through my life. Amen.

"OH, THAT. DAN'S BEEN FORGETTING
WHERE HE PUTS THINGS SO HE'S
STARTED VIDEO-TAPING HIS EVERY
MOVE."

LOVE MORE AND REGRET LESS

*Sometimes I make up my mind, other times my mind wanders,
and every so often I lose track of it entirely.*

I read somewhere that very few brain cells actually disappear in mid-life. But why then do I keep forgetting where I put my list of things I'll forget unless I write them down? I'm all for nostalgia, but it's hard to be nostalgic when you can't remember anything. At least memory loss helps me dispense with regret and guilt. I'm moving on, anticipating where I'm heading, open to today's answers to today's problems.

Some people pause to reminisce and then get stuck there. But I won't let my mistakes beat me up. So what if I missed while shooting for the moon? At least I journeyed for a while among the stars. And what if I did bite off more than I could chew? At least I cut a few wisdom teeth. Nowadays I may be slowing down, but I am definitely not settling back. I keep trying, just as my first-grade teacher taught me to do. And if at first I *do* succeed, I'll try not to look astonished.

How will the Lord use your life this year? This month? This day? Is there one thing you can do to make life better for someone else? Can you warm the home of an elderly friend?

Chill out so a teenager can open up to your love? Knock on the door of a lonely single mom? Invite a seven-year-old for lemonade? The possibilities are endless. God expects us to use our brains and figure out what we can do to make a difference. Find out where He's working and join His crew.

When we bring sunshine into the lives of others, we're warmed by it ourselves. When we spill a little happiness, it splashes on us. Hope uncovers new possibilities and shows us what can be done. It wrestles with angels, looks impossibilities in the eye and winks. Hope springs eternal. Hope supersedes all good intentions.

Positive thinking, on the other hand, can get you only so far. When that train of thought won't get you further, jump track and keep going by the power of God's grace. After all, you know Immanuel, God who is with us. Dare to believe that He has planned greater things right around the corner for the ones you love. Hold your loved ones before the throne and count on God's answer in their lives. Don't let your ability or inability to think your way around circumstances hold you back. Pray and rest. Then pray some more.

Today make a decision to be less afraid than you were yesterday. To love more than last week. To regret less than last year. To move forward in good deeds. Be forgetful of the past. Remember to do all the good you can do in all the ways you can do, ever as long as you can. And you can!

UPLIFTER

Now to him who is able to do immeasurably more than all we ask or imagine, according to his power that is at work within us, to him be glory.

EPHESIANS 3:20–21

WAY TO PRAY

Dear Lord, You are the great mind behind the universe. You made everything move according to Your timetable and plan. Please forgive me when I fret and stew. Please help me move into my future, all the while helping other people and accomplishing Your will. Amen.

THE BOOMERANG PRINCIPLE

Everybody wants to go to heaven,
but nobody wants to go there right away.

Don't we all want to live a long and happy life? We want as many years as possible to breathe, laugh, and work, serving God and praying for His kingdom to come. Along with this we'd like as many pleasant memories as possible, starting as early as possible. Youngsters, full of ambition, want to fulfill their destinies before the Lord returns. The middle-aged want to complete their life calling and make peace with troublesome people and issues. Older people want to see their lives come full circle before they die; they want to watch grandchildren grow up, graduate, marry, and have children.

No matter how old we are, most of us never really think of ourselves as old. Psychologists say most elderly people feel about thirty-two inside. (So Jack Benny was just a few years off!) Although our bodies betray us, our spirits often become more energized and focused as we age, and there is always too much left to do at the end of every life.

Somehow we must make peace with what we won't be able to accomplish. To do that, it helps to think of the things you probably can accomplish. What twenty goals would you like to reach before you exit planet Earth? If you are going to live until you die, you may as well arrange in advance for pleasant memories.

Every good life is a balance of duty and bliss. We will be called upon to do things we would rather not. Sometimes people say, "Just follow your heart," but that isn't necessarily the right approach. We have to weigh decisions by mind and spirit and by the Word of God. Whether you live to be nineteen or ninety, life is still short. Even the oldest, wisest man is amazed by its brevity. So make each year count. Instead of clutching it fast, give it away. "Cast your bread upon the waters" (Eccl. 11:1) and it comes back pretzels! That's the heart of the boomerang principle.

Do you have a gift for making people laugh? Writing a short story? Baking a great loaf of bread? Do you listen well? Throw a mean softball? Can you organize anything with flair? Are you good at making money? Selling just about anything? Running a race? Put yourself in the center ring. Offer your energy to life and do it heartily, unto the Lord.

Don't forget to celebrate anything you can think of. Do things that make you aware of how great it is to be alive. Every day is worth a party, not just the cookie-cutter moments. Special occasions are everywhere. Don't always be practical and expedient. God gave us license to be outrageously happy, friendly, and rejoicing.

- Celebrate your health if it's good this month.
- Celebrate that you came through another year without a car accident.

- Celebrate wildflowers springing through the earth, the first robin in your yard, the first snowfall, the first good haircut you've had in years.
- Invite friends or strangers to celebrate with you. Look for original gifts you can give.

A couple of years ago a darling lady wrote to say she wanted to give me a birthday gift. For an entire year she would act as my "clipper." She was going to clip cartoons, articles, jokes, and other stuff for my newsletter, anything that would help my ministry. I thought, *What a wonderful idea.* So for several months I received a packet from her on the first day of every month. It was fabulous! All the cartoons and special articles came in so handy in putting together the newsletter.

Each month I eagerly awaited the packet, marveling at how she had taken the time to give me this special gift. Then suddenly the packets stopped arriving, and I learned that this thoughtful lady had died. But her idea blossomed. When my special doctor friend had his birthday that year, I was stumped about what to give him. Knowing he wouldn't need anything I could buy him, I decided that for one year my gift would be to clip out all the articles I could find relating to his specialty. In addition to his own studies, I thought he'd like to read what his patients were reading.

My husband got me a little clipping instrument to carry in my purse when I travel. I looked in magazines and newspapers for articles on health issues that would be of interest to my doctor. At beauty shops or dentist offices, too, I found great articles and information. Collecting the clippings in a bright neon envelope each month, I added enticing candy bars, sticks of gum, or whimsical candies so he had something to munch on as he read the material. Then I enclosed a funny card. My doctor enjoyed the package, and I learned a lot by investing my energy this way. It has boomeranged back into my life. What started out as a simple gesture to give has blessed and been a joy to me.

You can implement low-cost ideas to cheer the lives of people in your life: the baby-sitter, the postman, your favorite grocery clerk or carry-out boy. When you visit a home with small children, splurge on things that make kids' eyes shine. You don't even have to wrap them. Bring a deck of cards, a ball to toss, a Frisbee or jump rope. Get involved in their games.

Keep looking for ways to bless others. Compete with yourself to see if you can find more creative ways to love this week than last. Brainstorm blessing projects for next year. The point is to live every single day as though it were your last. Because if you do that, one day you'll be right!

UPLIFTER

He who refreshes others will himself be refreshed.
PROVERBS 11:25

WAY TO PRAY

Heavenly Father, help me not to count my days but to daily count the ways I can share life with other people. Amen.

525,600 MINUTES
TO ENJOY

*Be happy today, right now—while there's still time—
because today never becomes tomorrow.*

A man walked into a bookstore and while browsing, mentioned to the owner that he'd just thrown away an old Bible he'd found somewhere. "It was in a foreign language anyway, printed somewhere like Guten . . . ," he said.

"Not Gutenberg?" gasped the bookstore owner.

"Yes, that was it," the man replied.

"You may have thrown away a book worth four hundred thousand dollars, one of the first books ever printed!"

"Aw, it wouldn't be worth a dime," the man responded. "Some guy by the name of Martin Luther had scribbled all over its pages."

You never know what life is going to turn up! The most significant people are scribbling all over the pages of your life today, right now. Don't let pearls slip between your fingers. Look at the life you hold in your own two hands. Is it tattered and shabby? Think about it. Might it bring opportunities for growth and gladness? Might it be treasure? What is going to be important one hundred years from now that doesn't seem important now? What seems important now that will not be important a century from now?

In moments that appear unredeemable, watch and wait. Recognize the precious things. Refuse to trash anything! Ask God to help you see things from His perspective. Take one step after another. Before long, in spite of yourself, you may notice surprising signs of hope in your own backyard: the chuckle of a baby, the kindly light in a neighbor's eyes, the sweet kiss of a spouse, an undreamed of opportunity.

The best thing about this very minute is your ability to recognize the possibilities in it. Any fool can count the seeds in an apple. But only God can count the apples in a seed. There is something in every problem that holds potential for something better. Do you want a lifetime of happy *right nows?* The little choice this moment to see the beauty in what appears ugly, frustrating, or disgraceful will change everything. You have 1,440 minutes in every day. That's 525,600 minutes per year!

But what happens when things go wrong—like, really wrong? Several years ago my brother-in-law, Mel, visited just after I had purchased newfangled hair clippers to give my boys haircuts. The clippers had a neat little plastic gauge that fit over the blade to determine the exact length of the cut. You simply adjusted it and then just sort of mowed the hair, or so I thought! Somehow I persuaded Mel to be my first customer.

Poor Mel. It was a disaster! I had plowed furrows on top of his head and scraggly patterns on each side. Fortunately, he is a good sport. Leaving on a train for Minneapolis the next day, he pulled his hat so far down over his head, it hid everything

"OK, WHAT'D YOU DO WITH MY BOTTLE
COLLECTION?!"

but his nose and chin. As I waved him off, he laughed and hollered, "Don't worry, it'll grow back!"

Afterward I thought about how those words apply to life. Mel's response comes back to me whenever I feel that life's circumstances seem as treacherous as those hair clippers. God's promises hold true when everything around me changes. Knowing this helps me treasure exactly what I have and where I am, even amid disaster. Hair grows or falls out. Hairstyles change. Color jobs fade. Even permanents aren't permanent! So many things seem important only after I've lost them: a certain someone, good health, hope.

The time to be happy is *now*. The thing to treasure is exactly what you hold in your hands. No matter how you try to manipulate reality—forcing changes, denying what's true, worrying about tomorrow—it is only by accepting life as it is today that you will become truly rich.

Trial and triumph are what God uses to scribble all over the pages of our lives. They are signs that He is using us, loving us, shaping us to His image, enjoying our companionship, delivering us from evil, and writing eternity into our hearts. Be happy through everything because today is the only thing you can be sure of. Right here, right now, cherish the moment you hold in your hands.

UPLIFTER

See, I have engraved you on the palms of my hands; your walls are ever before me.

ISAIAH 49:16

WAY TO PRAY

O Lord! How thankful I am for Your permanence and Your unfathomable love in my process of change. As You retool my life to make me more useful, help me appreciate the changes that come. Help me to be glad for every *right now* moment! Amen.

ALL MY MARBLES

The end is not near; you must learn to cope.

Whenever my husband, Bill, and I travel to speaking engagements, we take along several pounds of iridescent glass marbles, piling them up in the middle of our book table. The marbles are actually flat, about the size of a half-dollar, with smooth, rounded edges. They come in rainbow colors: red, lilac, blue, amber, purple, and green. When placed in the light, the marbles reflect it and seem to shimmer, so we call them splashes of joy. In the middle of the marbles we put a small sign that says, "This is your free splash of joy. Place it on a windowsill where the sun will hit it . . . and it will remind you of all the places God wants to bless you!" There must be more than a ton of those sparkling iridescent splashes in circulation by now.

One day when I had finished arranging the table and was leaving to take my place on the podium, I said to the volunteer selling my books, "Remember, the splashes of joy are free; everybody can take one." Later when I returned to the book table, I saw dozens of ladies in the foyer walking around with my book *Splashes of Joy in the Cesspools of Life*. I thought, *Wow, that book certainly sold well today, but I wonder why so many people bought that one?* (I had seven others on sale, too.)

Noticing five or six empty boxes under the book table, I asked the volunteer about it. She said, "Oh, you said all the *Splashes of Joy* were free, so I let everyone take one!"

Uh-oh!

I hope those *Splashes of Joy* became showers of blessing to the many who picked them up that day. I did laugh about the incident ... later, that is. Joy really is a take-it-or-leave-it kind of thing. My glass marbles remind me that the choice is always mine. I can choose whether to shine and sparkle or sit and stew.

Whenever child star Shirley Temple got up to perform, her mother would always say, "Sparkle, Shirley!" And (since I'm the same age as Shirley) I took those words to heart. That day at the book table I heard the Holy Spirit whisper, "Sparkle, Barbara, sparkle!"

When the devastating earthquake struck southern California in 1994 (they said it wasn't the "big one," but it was big enough for me!), one woman wrote to tell me how her little "sparkle stone," as she called it, helped her keep smiling through her tears. She wrote,

About a year ago I attended a retreat where you were the speaker, and you gave each lady some sparkle stones to take home and put on a windowsill. I did. Then I kind of forgot about them. But their message of Jesus' love came to me as I was cleaning a huge mess of broken things after the earthquake.

The refrigerator and all the cupboards had opened and emptied, and everything had broken into millions of pieces. I was sad, scared, and upset as I cleaned. Then I saw a "sparkle" among my broken treasures. I cried as I scooped up the little sparkle stone and thanked God that I had been able to have those treasures for the years I had enjoyed them. I thought, "For this I have Jesus." When I saw that sparkle stone, I had to smile and say, "Thank you, Barbara, for this reminder that Jesus loves me. I'll sparkle for Him."

Remember this story; don't miss the beautiful colors of the rainbow while you're looking for the pot of gold at the end of it! When your life comes to a close, you will remember not days but moments. Treasure each one. And know that the most glorious of these are not the so-called moments of success and accomplishment but rather those moments when out of dejection and despair you let rise within you the promise of joy!

The glass marbles we give away remind me why I go out to speak: we are put on this earth not to see through each other but to see each other through. I want to help see others through their pain. I want to throw a little encouragement party. I want others to be drenched with joy. That's what makes it all worthwhile.

When the marbles are first shipped to me from the manufacturer, they are bundled in small nets and covered with a powder residue that prevents them from scratching during shipping. If I want them to be lustrous and transparent when we hand them out, I have to undo each bundle, place the marbles in the kitchen sink, rinse them off, then spread them out on a towel to dry.

One day when I was home, busy at this task, a newspaper reporter called. She said she was calling various authors to find out precisely what they were doing at that exact moment. Wondering how this was going to sound, I answered, "Well, I'm washing my marbles—in the sink."

The reporter didn't answer for a moment. Then she asked, "Who is this again?"

"It's Barbara Johnson."

"The Christian author?"

"Well, yes!"

"And you're washing your marbles?"

By this time she must have thought she'd dialed the wrong number and reached the home for the hopelessly bewildered. But she laughed as I explained that I always rinse the splashes of joy before giving them away. Then I told her that washing my marbles helps me remember how God washes us and cleans us up. His love rinses away the residue we pick up trying to protect ourselves from life's scratchy circumstances. When He is finished with us, we are shining, transparent and lustrous.

Many of my friends know I love to joke about my marbles—about washing them and occasionally "losing" them. In fact, one friend sent me a little plaque titled "All My Marbles Certificate." It said, "This is to certify that I, Barbara Johnson, am in possession of All My Marbles. I can never again be accused of not having All My Marbles." At the bottom of the certificate, this zany friend had written, "If everyone had All Their Marbles, the world would be a nicer place to live!"

Sometimes I do lose my marbles; my mind wanders—or it leaves completely. But that's OK. The marbles I have left remind me of the light of God's plan and how wonderful it is to be alive. I've decided to enjoy today's moments today, because someday today will be a long time ago. I know a lady whose mother died in her arms of breast cancer shortly before this lady herself was scheduled for a double mastectomy. A survivor of breast cancer for several years now, she says with a smile, "Even on bad days, I am so happy! To think I'm even here to have a bad day cheers me up!"

Certainly the rain falls on the just and the unjust (chiefly on the just, because the unjust steal their umbrellas). But a few splashes of pain don't get me down for long. In the cesspools of life, I remember the colorful splashes of joy on my windowsill. I take my rainbow with me and share it with others! We cannot protect ourselves from trouble, but we can dance through the puddles of life with a rainbow smile, twirling the only umbrella we need—the umbrella of God's love. His covering of grace is sufficient for any problem we may have.

UPLIFTER

Cleanse me with hyssop, and I will be clean; wash me, and I will be whiter than snow. Let me hear joy and gladness. . . . Create in me a pure heart, O God.

PSALM 51:7–8, 10

WAY TO PRAY

Dear Lord, You have sprinkled splashes of joy throughout my moments and my days. When I look back, I see Your patterns of color and meaning, shimmering just like a rainbow. You are beautiful, God, and You make my life beautiful, too, as You wash me whiter than snow. Amen.

BIRTHDAY COUNTDOWN

The scary thing about middle age is the knowledge that you'll soon grow out of it.

Andy was miffed when he didn't get the part he wanted in the Christmas pageant. He had hoped for the role of Joseph but got stuck being the innkeeper. So Andy decided to pull a fast one and get even with Joseph when he came with Mary, looking for a place to stay.

"Come right in, folks," innkeeper Andy told them. "I've got plenty of room."

Perplexed, Mary looked at the startled Joseph, who quickly rose to the occasion.

"Hey, this place is a real dump," he said, poking his head inside. "I'd rather go out and sleep in the stable."

Whatever happened to the wit and wisdom that served us so well as kids? Why can't we use that when middle age baffles us? Experts say innate creativity begins to disappear at about age eleven because we stop using it. We become progressively less curious and spontaneous.

Youth is not a time of life but a state of mind. It boldly takes risks, seeks adventure, hopes for the best, and displays courage. You are as young as your faith is strong.

The actor Jimmy Stewart stayed young until the day he died at age eighty-nine. Although extraordinarily talented, he remained touched by the fact that he was a celebrity. One time a stranger put his hand out and said, "Mr. Stewart, I don't guess it means much to you, but I want you to know I think you're wonderful." Taking the man's hand to shake it, Jimmy held on to it tightly, looked him in the eye, and said, "It means everything to me."

We live out the kingdom of God within us when we treasure each other like that and when we find ways to turn unfortunate things around. Laughter is one of those ways. Laughter stirs the blood, expands the chest, electrifies the nerves, and clears the cobwebs from the brain. If you laugh a lot, when you are older all your wrinkles will be in the right places!

If you live to be one hundred, your heart will have beat 3,681,619,200 times, pumping 27,323,260 gallons of blood weighing over one hundred tons. (If you end up tired, you've earned it!) Think about making every heartbeat a happy one.

Actually, I think living to be one hundred would be great, but living to fifty twice would be so much better. The way to do that is to get one year younger each year after your fiftieth birthday. So on your fifty-first birthday you turn forty-nine, at sixty you are forty, and so on. I'm not saying lie about your age; actually grow younger every year!

The first rule for this (you'll start looking younger, too) is to scatter joy to everyone you meet. There is no more effective beauty secret. The second rule is to exercise regularly—and the best heart workout is reaching down and lifting someone else up. The third and last rule is to guard your enthusiasm; in fact, let every experience in life multiply it. Every single experience! If someone leaves you only the shirt on your back, you have a choice: you can either use it for a crying towel or make a sail out of it. Go sailing, not ailing! And on your adventure at sea remember: the pessimist complains about the wind, the optimist expects the wind to change, but the spiritual man adjusts his sail.

One way of adjusting your sail as you travel through rough seas is to find fun in unlikely places. Sometimes you have to give yourself permission to have fun. You cannot trap fun like an animal or catch it like the flu. But if you go look-ing for it, it'll come. The magic of fun lies in the unexpected—whether chasing dreams, flying kites, or going up on the down escalator. Break out of your middle-age mold and become a little bit crazy—even if friends think you're fresh out of a rubber room!

You can't turn back the clock, of course, but you can wind it up again. As a recycled teenager, insanity may be your best means of relaxation. The secret of growing younger is counting blessings, not birthdays. Don't grow up; grow down. You'll know you're getting the idea when you begin buying cereal for the toy, not the fiber.

If you keep it up long enough, sooner or later you'll grow down from teenager to toddler. Uh-oh, there is one thing about being a two-year-old that could take all the fun out of getting younger. Beware the toddlers' creed: *If I want it, it's mine. If it looks like mine, it is mine. If I take it away from you, it's mine. If I had it a little while ago, it's mine. If I give it to you and change my mind, it's mine.* No wisdom there; this breaks every rule of growing down. Skip this stuff, then hop and jump to infancy—that blissful time when you have no more responsibility than to eat and sleep and bask in the love of your family. No one will blame you for an occasional wakeful night or fussy afternoon. Dependent on others, enjoy the minutes as they fall through the hours, on your way through eternity.

UPLIFTER

Do not worry about your life. . . . But seek his kingdom, and these things will be given to you as well.

LUKE 12:22, 31

WAY TO PRAY

Lord, show me how to become like a child again. Let's go roll in some meadows and giggle like a brook. Teach me the quiet simplicity of loving You. Amen.

READY FOR ANYTHING?

Prepare and prevent rather than repair and repent.

As mothers and wives, we spend many years with our children, teaching and preparing them for life—specifically, preparing them for school, friends, and social graces—and with husbands, who start as mavericks until we train them to become thoroughbreds. But with all the time and energy we expend teaching our family these things, no one is standing in the wings to instruct *us* about anything. No one prepares us for the situations that come in our lives. *No one!*

Recently a friend sent me this bit about how to *prepare for a mammogram!* Since then I have shared it in conferences and listened to the uproar of laughter—sharing this has *boomeranged* back to me the most overwhelming hilarity. So this is just my boomerang of fun to you. As you share this, you too will enjoy the genuine boomerang principle; as you make another one laugh, you yourself will enjoy the laughter!

THE MAMMOGRAM

This is an x-ray that has its own name because no one wants to actually *say* the word "breast." Mammograms require your breasts to do gymnastics. If you have extremely agile breasts, you should do fine. Most breasts, however, pretty much hang around doing nothing in particular, so they are woefully unprepared. But you can prepare for a mammogram right at home using these simple exercises.

Exercise 1: Refrigerate two bookends overnight. Lay one of your breasts (either will do) between the two bookends and *smash* the bookends together as hard as you can. Repeat this three times daily.

Exercise 2: Locate a pasta maker or old wringer washer. Feed the breast into the machine and start cranking. Repeat twice daily.

Exercise 3. (*advanced only please*) Situate yourself comfortably on your side on the garage floor. Place one of your breasts snugly behind the rear tire of the family van. When you give the signal, have your hubby slowly ease the car into reverse. Hold for five seconds. Repeat on the other side.

Share this with every woman you can think of. Then take a copy to your local women's clinic and share it with the nurses, doctors, and technicians. Next year, when mammogram time rolls around, make appointments at the same time as your best friend—or two—and throw a mammogram party with favors and treats for everyone who works at the clinic.

Always be prepared, and help others prepare, to turn the awkward situations of life into whimsical opportunities for celebration. Engage in boomerang joy in the most unusual places!

UPLIFTER

And do not forsake your mother's teaching.

PROVERBS 1:8

WAY TO PRAY

My dear heavenly Father, you have given us plenty of grist for joy in the middle of our pain. You have blessed us with creativity and resources for turning our lemons into lemonade. Help me always walk on the bright side of the street. Help me always find reasons laugh and be able to laugh at myself! Amen.

DIAMOND DUST

A gem cannot be polished without friction. Neither can a joy gem!

One day a man was walking down the street, when he passed a jewelry store. Stopping to admire the display in the window, he noticed the jeweler take yellowish diamonds and place them in a machine. Moments later as he watched, the jeweler took the diamonds out again. They were transparent now, without a yellow tinge. The man entered the shop, curious about the process.

"It's diamond dust" the jeweler said. "Only a diamond can cut another diamond. We use diamond dust to polish away the outer film, allowing a diamond's inner brilliance to shine through."

Brilliance. Shine. Transparency. Only God can transform a sin-stained soul into a masterpiece of grace. Jesus is the Rock of Ages, and the Holy Spirit is our engagement promise. He is preparing us now for that day when we will outshine all the gold of heaven, using diamond dust to polish away the stuff that hides His shimmer.

Trials are not enemies of faith but opportunities to reveal God's faithfulness. Someday we'll each have a gold star with our name engraved on it—not on the Hollywood walk of fame but embedded in those crystal streets of the new Jerusalem. And every week the angels will come and shine it up to show God's affection for us.

I read about a man who discovered a star somewhere in our universe and named it after himself. Now he is selling property on that star—divided into one-acre lots. With the sales deed you get to boast that your name is on a star. Sales are booming. (Sometimes I think stardust gets into people's brains and jams the circuits.) The good news is, we don't have to spend money for one-acre lots on stars in outer space. We've already got a reservation at the greatest resort in the cosmos. If our names are written in the Lamb's Book of Life, we lay claim to heaven itself rather than just one itty-bitty lot on one teeny-tiny star.

Life is a refining process. Our response to it determines whether we'll be ground down or polished up. On a piano, one person sits down and plays sonatas, while another merely bangs away at "Chopsticks." The piano is not responsible. It's how you touch the keys that makes the difference. It's how you play what life gives you that determines your joy and shine.

True, life sometimes makes you feel you're being tumbled in a cement mixer rather than a diamond polisher. But how you respond will either bring inner qualities to light or leave a dull finish. Joy is a by-product not of happy circumstances, education, or talent but of a healthy relationship with God and a determination to love Him no matter what.

When "Whatever, Lord!" replaces "Why me?" you know you are on your way through whatever diamond dust clouds your vision. When God measures your stature in the kingdom, He will weigh not your achievements or accomplishments but the brilliance of your soul. Even through wet tears your eyes will glisten. God will fashion your life to reflect His Son's glory. Life's storms will create a rainbow that brightens the lives of others.

It would be so easy if our lives were like VCRs so we could fast-forward through the crummy times. But we can't. Instead we need to live our stories moment by moment, day by day. As you do, refuse to give in to the diamond dust blues!

UPLIFTER

> *. . . so that you may become blameless and pure, children of God without fault in a crooked and depraved generation, in which you shine like stars in the universe.*
>
> PHILIPPIANS 2:15

WAY TO PRAY

Lord, thank You for diamond dust! Without it I'd hate to think about where and how I might end up. You are fashioning me for glory. You are loving me through my trials—as Your precious gem. I love You, Lord, and am proud to be a jewel in Your crown. Amen.

POWER IN FORGIVENESS

It is better to forgive and forget than to resent and remember.

Have you heard of International Forgiveness Week? Sure enough, I found it on the calendar, smack-dab in the middle of winter. In winter you feel dull and drab and closed in, as though spring will never come. You are restless, cold, and irritable, the way you feel when you hold a grudge.

Forgiveness enables you to bury your grudge in icy earth. To put the past behind you. To flush resentment away by being the first to forgive. Forgiveness fashions your future. It is a brave and brash thing to do. The gutsiest decision you can make. Here's a daily plan for Forgiveness Week. (Hint: For best results, follow the plan fifty-two weeks out of the year!)

Monday: Forgive yourself.
Tuesday: Forgive your spouse.
Wednesday: Forgive your children.
Thursday: Forgive your parents.
Friday: Forgive your friends.
Saturday: Forgive your enemies.
Sunday: Forgive members and leaders of your church.

As you forgive others, winter will soon make way for springtime as fresh joy pushes up through the soil of your heart.

Maybe you are the one who needs to be forgiven by others. You may feel that your sins are heaped to the skies:

FOREVER WORTHY

> *Dear God*
> *I have sinned*
> *Against Heaven*
> *And against You.*
> *I am no longer worthy*
> *To be called Your child.*
> *Child, I know . . . I know . . .*
> *But my Son*
> *Is forever worthy*
> *To be called your Savior.*
> —RUTH HARMS CALKIN

Do you live with regret because you compare what is with what might have been? Have you failed to do something you desperately wish you would have done? For every choice you made, you gave up a host of other choices. You know you cannot go back and unscramble eggs. You can't undo what has been done. Instead you must learn to make soufflés:

Monday: Build a bridge; do something good for someone else.
Tuesday: See past mistakes through the prism of humor.
Wednesday: Seize every moment; make more of opportunity.
Thursday: Surrender the need to always be right.
Friday: Reframe your circumstances; see them in a new light.
Saturday: Accept personal limitations, but give up self-blame.
Sunday: Change your priorities to avoid future omissive sins.

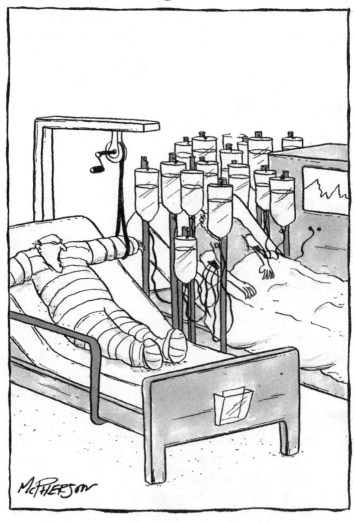

"WILL YOU QUIT WHISTLING
'DON'T WORRY, BE HAPPY'?!"

Forgiveness is a stunning principle, your ticket out of hate and fear and chaos. There are many ways to learn through pain and come to a place of acceptance. When I first discovered that one of my sons was gay, I felt crushed. We Christians think this sort of thing can never happen in our families, but I'm here to tell you it can. We've swept so many things under the rug that our rugs are lumpy. Many times I gave my son to God, then snatched back the burden until I was once again able to say the prayer of relinquishment—"Whatever, Lord"—and forgive. I know what regret feels like; I've earned my credentials. But I also know what forgiveness feels like, because God has so graciously forgiven me.

You can create self-respect by responding to your circumstances today in a way that will make you feel proud tomorrow. Forgiveness frees you of the past so you can make good choices today. Look to Jesus as your example. He was nailed to a cross between the two thieves so you and I could stop nailing ourselves to a cross between two other thieves—regret for yesterday and fear for tomorrow.

As with most things, laughter makes the work of forgiveness easier. Last year, the day the planets were supposed to line up and the world blow up—you remember that day, don't you?—Bill came in early, waking me from a sound sleep. He announced that the water heater was leaking all over the floor. My first thoughts were hopeful ones: maybe the world would blow up after all, and I wouldn't need to fix the water heater! But no such luck.

Getting a plumber took a bit of doing. When he arrived and diagnosed the problem, he asked for three hundred dollars to fix it and wondered if I wanted a five- or ten-year warranty.

I replied, "Five years will be fine, because after that I don't expect to be around much longer!" He looked at me quizzically.

After the job was done, he walked to the kitchen table to write out the bill. Lying flat out in open view that day—right in front of him—was a cheap little rag book someone had sent me (I hope as a joke) entitled "How to Be a Happy Homosexual." The plumber saw it but never said a word. He just kept writing out his paperwork, then left with a funny look on his face.

Afterward I began to laugh. In fact, I laughed wildly all the way to the post office that day, thinking about that poor guy, what he must have thought, and what he would tell his wife about me. The embarrassing experience turned into an occasion for joy. The joke was on me! I forgave Bill for waking me, forgave myself for nearly coming unglued, and most of all I forgave the person who sent me that book! Trying times are no time to quit trying. My life's tragedies have become occasions for ministry, through the power of forgiveness and the rule of no regrets. So can yours!

UPLIFTER

Forgive us our sins, for we also forgive everyone who sins against us.
LUKE 11:4

WAY TO PRAY

Heavenly Father, teach me to forgive my enemies, my friends, and myself. I don't want to live with regret. Show me a way to rise above my circumstances. I will to do Your will. Amen.

GOTTA BE REAL

Someday I'm going to write a book called
Answers I Didn't Want to Hear to Questions I Never Asked.

A professor asked his students, "What is the greatest problem in our society—ignorance or apathy?"

One student replied for all: "I don't know and I don't care."

Sometimes I think the world responds much the same way to Christians' earnest efforts to share the gospel. It makes you wonder: Are we addressing issues that matter? Are we answering questions that no one is even asking? I saw a cartoon in which a man was standing on a street corner. Passersby were hurrying around him. He was throwing a tantrum, saying, "Doesn't anybody want to know the source of my inner peace?"

Another cartoon shows a man going through the express lane—"Twelve Items or Less"—at the grocery store. He witnesses to the checker: "For all have sinned . . ." The checker replies nonchalantly, "Includin' you, Mac. I count fourteen items here!"

Do we want people to listen? We gotta be real. If we want to spread hope and joy, if we want people to know our Lord and Savior Jesus Christ, let's stop faking who we are. The only

"THAT'S ONE OF THE THINGS I LOVE
ABOUT JERRY; HE'S A GREAT
LISTENER."

thing that's separating *them* from *us* is that we are forgiven. Our problems are no less tragic. Our lives no less complicated. Our children no less wayward. Our futures no more safe or secure. Our mates no more faithful. Our burdens no less heavy. For all of us life is mostly a struggle to keep our weight down and our spirits up. The difference is that Christians have Someone who will go the distance with them.

In your desire to share the gospel, you may be the only Jesus someone else will ever meet. Be real and involved with people. They may be closer to the kingdom of heaven than you think. A good rule of thumb is to keep your heart a little softer than your head!

Let experience teach you to be real. Experience is what you get when you don't get what you want. There is only one thing more painful than learning from experience, and that is not learning from it! It's in the darkest places, after all, that the grace of God shines most brightly. That is where people begin to see Him. By His wounds we are healed. By our scars we are recognized as belonging to Him.

There is something about having endured great loss that brings purity of purpose and strength of character. So let's be who we are. No longer afraid of ourselves. No longer afraid of others.

Time mellows people as it mellows wine, as long as the grapes are good. You may set out to be a businesswoman but in the course of time end up caring for a dying parent, orphaned niece, or disabled brother. You may encounter illness yourself and end up being a writer, touching the heartstrings, not the purse strings, of other people. That's why it's best to always be true to yourself and God and to be flexible within His will. He will use you.

Remember, things will turn out all right, but sometimes it takes strong nerves just to watch the circumstances unfold. Take a moment now to reflect on the promises God has given. Meditate on hope and the opportunities for growth that have come to you in pain. Think about the talents with which God has gifted you. Ask the Holy Spirit to help you be genuine in all your relationships. Allow God to answer the world's questions through your life. Your life is the real work, after all—and the reward for work well done is the opportunity to do even more!

UPLIFTER

The greatest among you will be your servant. For whoever exalts himself will be humbled, and whoever humbles himself will be exalted.
MATTHEW 23:11–12

WAY TO PRAY

Lord, You've called me to a real world, not a fluffy cloud on which to play my harp. You've called me to be Your presence in the ugliest of places, to be Your hope in desperation. I need strength, Lord, and a firm footing. Help me never to answer questions that are not being asked but simply to be Jesus to another person today. Amen.

THE WINGS OF PRAYER

*Each of us are like angels with only one wing—
we can fly only by embracing another.*

During WWI a group of American soldiers were pinned down by heavy fire in a mud-filled trench somewhere in France. Their only hope was to somehow take the enemy bunker raking their position. Two men had died trying. The sergeant barked to a third, "Webster, you're up!" The soldier hesitated, pulled back the sleeve of his coat, and looked at his watch. "Get out there!" yelled the sergeant again. The soldier sucked in his breath and once more checked his watch. "This is an order! Get out there and throw your grenade in that bunker! Do you understand? This is an order!" shouted the sergeant. The trembling soldier bit his lip, pulled himself to the edge of the trench, and looked at his watch. Then, scrambling over fallen comrades, he dipped and dodged his way across the battle zone and collapsed at the edge of the bunker, shaking so badly he could barely jerk the pin from the grenade and throw it into the bunker.

When the enemy bunker exploded, the Americans charged. Later the sergeant pulled the soldier aside. "What were you waiting for?" he asked. "Why did you keep looking at your watch? Don't you understand what an order is?"

The soldier replied, "My mother promised to say a prayer for me every day at noon. I was waiting for twelve o'clock, that's all."

Every Christian, every single one of us, lives in the midst of spiritual warfare daily. But how often have you told someone, "I'll pray for you" and realized that their life may actually depend on it? For many, our basic to-do list consists of three points:

1. Get up.
2. Survive.
3. Go to bed.

The promise to pray for someone going through hard times rolls easily off our tongues. But do we really mean it? Our sisters, brothers, and children in the faith need our committed involvement in their lives.

Praying is not a way to gain control. It's just the opposite. We rely on God. We adopt His love on behalf of another person. We invite His power into another's life. Taking authority over all the power of the Enemy (Luke 10:19), we continue in our position as warriors. The answers are not ours to demand. We are merely to be faithful. Prayer is not a last resort but a first-rate privilege. We don't know how to pray as we ought, but we ought to pray anyway. As we pray, we may face finite disappointment, but we must never lose infinite hope.

In 1976 seven young women who worked for Campus Crusade for Christ were swept into a flash flood while in Colorado attending a conference. News of their deaths spread quickly as bodies were recovered from the river. One state away, in the tiny mining town of Pitcher, Oklahoma, a jubilant headline appeared in the local paper. Mary Graham had been traveling with the girls trapped in the raging river. Her large family was known and loved in the small community. The two-inch headline fairly shouted: "Mary Wasn't There!"

Mary was spared while seven other girls died in the flood. Surely everyone's families were praying. Why didn't all the girls survive? We never know why some things happen as they do. But we stand upon the rocky shores of life and keep on praying, because prayer changes the one who prays as much as it changes those for whom we pray. The truth is that God is shaping us all for higher things. And that is the greatest miracle of all.

A Jewish mother separated from her son scraped the words of a prayer into the wall of a boxcar bound for a Nazi concentration camp: "I am Hannah. My son is Ari. If you see him, tell him." Perhaps it was her last cry to the world and to God. That boxcar now stands in Jerusalem. On the wall of another place where the Jews hid in WW II was scrawled,

Believe in the sun even when it is not shining.
Believe in love even when it is not shown.
Believe in God even when He is silent.

This also is prayer—prayer for courage, hope, and faith. Was it answered? It is still being answered!

A little boy prayed, "Dear God, take care of the whole world. And please, God, take care of Yourself, or we're all sunk!"

Every day God is answering that prayer and millions of others. Some people think their prayers have fallen on deaf ears. But they have not. It takes faith to know that. Faith is the ability to let your light shine even after your fuse is blown.

97

Faith is seeing light with the eyes of your heart, when the eyes of your body see only darkness ahead.

In faithful prayer we embrace not only the people we love—we embrace God and His kingdom. We take flight. We are on our way somewhere. God is changing things through our willingness to pray and keep at it. While sorrow looks back and worry looks around, faith looks up. You are a child of God. Take wing!

UPLIFTER

But take heart! I have overcome the world.

JOHN 16:33

WAY TO PRAY

Dear God, I have only a small heart in which to carry my burdens. But I will bring it to You every day in prayer. Please use my tears and laughter, my love and compassion, to help someone else through this day. Amen.

JOY BEGETS JOY

Even if your life is full of cactus, you don't have to sit on it!

Experts tell us that both good news and bad news create stress. When you get a promotion, become engaged, or win the lottery, you enter the stress zone just as you do when you lose a job, divorce, or go bankrupt. Whether it is good stress or bad, experts advise people to put off decision making until things level out. Even in the midst of great joy, it's better not to make big promises.

Stress is confusion. It is being in a daze. Like jet lag, stress taps a high percentage of your mental and emotional energy. And it tests your character. No woman can know her true grit until she has run out of gas on the highway, purchased something on the installment plan, and reared a teenager. Yes, stress is everywhere. People stress out because they know today is the tomorrow they worried about yesterday—but not nearly enough!

Dieters know what stress is. Someone said, "I've been on a diet for two weeks, and all I've lost is fourteen days." That's self-imposed stress. Have you heard of the new Chinese diet? You can eat all you want, but you can only use one chopstick. Nondieters know stress, too. I read about a woman who collected T-shirts wherever she traveled. A friend asked her one day, "Whatever happened to that T-shirt you got in New Orleans? You know, the one that says, 'Life is short. Eat dessert first.'" Chagrined, the woman replied, "Well, I had to give that one away. It got too tight!"

Lots of money or lack of it can also create stress, say experts. (I guess most of us know more about the latter than the former.) A young woman once asked God how long a million years was to Him. God replied, "A million years to Me is just like a single second in your time." The woman asked what a million dollars was to Him. He said, "A million dollars to Me is just like a single penny to you." The young woman got up her courage and asked, "God, could I have one of Your pennies?" God smiled and replied, "Certainly, just a second!"

What happens when you think you are winning the rat race and along come faster rats? How do you deal with the stress? Remember those little yellow happy faces that say, "Smile"? For a while they went out of style because people thought they were trite. Now researchers are finding just the opposite. They say that even when you don't feel like it, smiling actually lifts your spirits and relieves stress. In one study, subjects were asked to hold a pen lightly in their teeth. Those who were told not to let their lips touch the pen—and therefore had to smile inadvertently—reported being in a better mood than those who kept their lips closed. Try it and see!

Or try popping a peppermint! The scent affects the same nerve that responds to smelling salts, enhancing alertness and energy. Vanilla works in the opposite manner to bring soothing, relaxing feelings to the surface; you can find this scent in all kinds of lotions, colognes, and bath gels. But the best advice for stress is this: you may not be able to avoid suffering, but you don't have to wallow it in. Pain comes into everybody's life, but misery is optional. Stress may be a given factor, but your attitude can change the way it affects you.

Stress is nothing but psychological pollution. Somebody once defined stress as the confusion created when the mind overrides the body's desire to choke the living daylights out of some jerk who desperately needs it! Flush stuff like that out of your system with a positive outlook. Keep mentally limber; accept what you can't change, and don't dwell on your own or others' shortcomings. Debrief by sharing your feelings with a trusted friend. Take a nap, time-out, or a walk by yourself. Be an imp for a day or an hour, make a neighbor laugh, play a practical joke, delight yourself with a wacky surprise. A chuckle is the soul's way of sneezing.

The experts (you know, those people who assign points to every stressful event in your life) also say that for every stressful event, you need at least four positive experiences to overcome it. Since it's so difficult to make good things happen (you can't just reel them in), the best way to overcome the bad stuff is to find reasons to be thankful. Don't waste today's time cluttering up tomorrow's opportunities with yesterday's troubles!

Ultimately things work out best for those who make the best of the way things work out. Stay cool. And while you're at it, try doing something outrageously nice the next time you are under stress. (Flowers and chocolate are always good choices!) God has promised to turn your "hours of stressing into showers of blessing." Be patient. Then choose: gather disappointment, loneliness, failure—or a bouquet of grace, love, and joy. The end may not be near, so you've got to learn to cope. And remember, nobody can get your goat if you don't tell where you tied it!

UPLIFTER

For everyone born of God overcomes the world. This is the victory that has overcome the world, even our faith.

1 JOHN 5:4

WAY TO PRAY

Dear God, it seems everyone is so stressed-out these days that I have nowhere to turn for comfort in my difficulties. But I know You are there for me. Please, Lord, give me strength enough not only to deal with my own issues but to reach out and help someone else with theirs. Amen.

MAKING LIFE *BEARABLE*

I wonder . . . do kamikaze pilots wear helmets?

I grew up taking risks. In fact, I've always thought success and risk go hand in hand. My motto is that people who live in a dangerous world ought to live dangerously. Of course I don't advocate taking foolish risks, but neither should we play it so safe that our lives are boring and our spirits dull.

Most of us are bombarded by daily warnings: buckle up, button up, watch for bumps ahead. We need brake checks, breast checks, dental checks, and Pap smears; medical insurance, disability insurance, life insurance, car insurance, mortgage insurance, and nursing home insurance. On and on. If we were to do everything everybody told us, we'd spend every minute of our waking day trying to prevent calamity.

I figure you may succeed in living longer if you're willing to stop doing everything that makes you want to live longer. I know someone intent on living forever, a vegetarian non-smoker who moved to the country, where there was plenty of fresh air, healthy water, and no industrial waste. Sadly, he died in a car accident when he was only thirty-eight. The real

"OK, YOU CAN COME OUT. I GOT RID OF THE BAT."

tragedy is not that life ends so soon but that we wait so long to begin it.

Life *is* dangerous. All of us are on a kamikaze mission. Not one of us will make it out alive. Should we wear helmets? I don't know about you, but I refuse to play it safe. I'll drop goodness and joy as many places as possible before my time comes to say *sayonara*. The best any of us can do is to show unconditional love to family, friends, and strangers. The best we can do is to encourage faith without excluding fun and laughter. To bring the gospel and the love of Jesus into the lives of everybody we meet.

The best we can do is to live until we die, a life that is bold and true and fun. Maybe that's why I've put bears on my stationary. I send out so many notes—short, encouraging messages to people going through long, discouraging trials. Scripture tells us to bear with one another (Col. 3:13) and to bear one another's burdens (Gal. 6:2). On my notes, one bear is hugging another, and the logo says, "I wish I could hug away your hurt, but I hope it helps to know I care." I hope the bears remind everybody that nothing in this dangerous world is unbearable, because the Lord promised not to give you more trouble than you can bear (1 Cor. 10:13).

Worry never empties tomorrow of its sorrow, but it does empty it of its strength. Don't let anyone rob you of your confidence in God. Know His Word. Hold on to His hand. He will make your impossible mission possible and your life so much more than bearable.

"ALL I CAN MAKE OUT IS 'CIRCUS' AND 'CANNON.'"

UPLIFTER

For he will command his angels concerning you to guard you in all your ways; they will lift you up in their hands.

PSALM 91:11–12

WAY TO PRAY

Dear Lord, Your own Son lived dangerously so I might enjoy abundant life. Help me to live that life to the full, gladly embracing the risks You place in my path. Amen.

THE BIG JOY ROOM—
IN THE SKY

My idea of housework is to sweep the room with a glance.

Whenever I'm not on the road, the things that consume me most are the mail and the telephone. Mail to Spatula Ministries is collected in large rectangular tubs that we pick up at the post office. (Our address should be a P.O. *tub* number rather than a box number because *box* doesn't begin to describe the barrel-size bin where our mail ends up.) I try to respond to letters with a phone call because it's so much faster. At the same time, I exercise on a bike set up in my joy room, a room filled with anything funny I've ever collected or been given: plaques, toys, gadgets, hats, and goofy things. Right in front of my bike I've posted a large map of the U.S. As I cycle, I mark my progress by sticking a pin into the map every twenty-five miles. That way I take imaginary trips across the country while talking on the phone, answering letters in a roomful of joy-filled gizmos!

My life is filled with people now, just like it was when I was at home rearing four boys. At that time I started a practice of taking the first day of each month off, making it a day just for myself. I still do this and find it helps me keep everything else in perspective. Just knowing I have one day a month all to myself keeps me grounded and motivated.

Still, there are days when I start feeling blue. On those days I've learned to avoid certain things. I won't weigh myself, listen to sad music, get a haircut, open a box of chocolates, or shop for a bathing suit. Instead on such days I make it a goal to perk up and be happy. The best way is to become a joy germ carrier. Infecting people with joy so they break out in symptoms of laughter—that's the very best way to beat the blues.

My joy habit has turned into a hobby. Sometimes I think up crazy bumper sticker ideas inspired by crazier ones like this: "Husband and dog missing. Reward for dog." Other times I create cards with uplifting themes. As my friend Faye Angus says: "We can't all be stars, but we can all twinkle." Or I might just call a friend and ask profound questions:

- Would a fly without wings be called a walk?
- Is it possible to be totally partial?
- Do they sterilize needles for lethal injections?
- Can you be a closet claustrophobic?

Women love jokes about dieting, aging, and men (those creatures God gave to us so we'd always have something to laugh about). These have become favorite themes for me to write and talk about in a spirit of fun. When I travel, I combine all three themes, struggling to eat sensibly despite lavish hotel menus, keeping up with schedules made for twenty-year-olds, and flying cross-country with my husband, Bill, at my side. Both of us have learned to laugh about things that go wrong along the way, realizing that life is nothing at all like the brochure.

I've made it a habit to wring out of every single day all the fun and love I can find. If you don't know where to start next time you're feeling low, take it simply:

7:00 Get up, don your makeup, and dress up for breakfast.

8:00 Show up for work with a big smile on your lips.

10:00 Take a coffee break and pass out crazy-flavored jelly beans.

12:00 Invite a friend to lunch.

2:00 Call your spouse, a child, or a friend and make a date for the weekend.

4:00 Order a bouquet of flowers delivered to your neighbor's door.

6:00 Put candles on the dinner table and turn on the music.

8:00 Design a funny card and send it to your aunt or mother.

10:00 Belt out your favorite gospel song in the shower and memorize a Scripture promise before you turn out the light.

After you get the basics down, you can fill in the hours with crazy excursions into comedy. You'll learn what makes people laugh and how to communicate through chuckles. The point is simply to get started. The point is never to give up. The point is to be friendly and to focus on the person next to you. There are two ways to come into a room: "Hey! Here I am!" or "Oh! There you are!" People who like people are people that people like! It's as simple as that.

Boomerang Joy

One of the best ways to encourage someone who's hurting is with your ears—by listening. But it's so much harder than talking. And few people do it well. A good listener not only is in demand everywhere but after a while actually knows something.

Mother Teresa pointed out that the great tragedy of life is not hunger or disease but feeling unwanted. This tragedy is as prevalent in America as in India. Everywhere, abandoned, isolated people ache with loneliness. As you're rushing through life, take time to stop a moment, look into people's eyes, say something kind, and try to make them laugh! Tell them life is easier than they think: a person need only accept the impossible, do without the indispensable, bear the intolerable, and be able to smile at anything!

Recently Bill and I stayed at a lovely old bed-and-breakfast inn loaded with antiques. In our room, hanging by the bed, was a long stick with a sort of bellows on the end. The hostess told us it was a quilt fluffer. You slide it inside the covers and pump it a few times to make the bed softer. Maybe we all need something like a quilt fluffer to buoy up our sagging, smasheddown world. We've been sitting on each other for far too long.

Try it. Fluff things up a bit or pretend for a moment that you're a star—then go ahead and poke a hole in someone else's darkness!

UPLIFTER

... that they may be encouraged in heart and united in love, so that they may have the full riches of complete understanding, in order that they may know the mystery of God, namely, Christ, in whom are hidden all the treasures of wisdom and knowledge.

COLOSSIANS 2:2–3

WAY TO PRAY

Dear heavenly Father, surely Your kingdom will be like a great big joy room where we will gather with You. Meanwhile help me to cast the bread of happiness and laughter on the waters of this world. I love You and wait expectantly for the adventures You send me to. Amen.

CRAZY QUILT

I love you more than yesterday.
Yesterday you really got on my nerves!

I like to think of my family as a big, beautiful patchwork quilt—each of us so different yet stitched together by love and life experiences. We are different textures: smooth and soft, rough and sturdy, bright and sparkly, subdued and peaceful. If one square is worn, others are there to hold the quilt together.

Patchwork blankets tell stories. How many women have treasured the work, passing it from generation to generation? The blue patch may have been the pocket of Great-Grandmother's dress, the tiny square of pink from the blouse of an aunt who died of smallpox, the little triangles of corduroy from the knickers Great-Uncle Joe wore playing that newfangled game called baseball. What transpired in the family while the blanket was being pieced together? Were they traveling west on a wagon train or huddling before a coal fire in the Appalachians?

Family quilts are an affirmation of the past, present, and future. They reassure us with their warmth, and comfort us with memories of hard times that turned out well.

For generations mothers and grandmothers have given a cherished quilt to daughters on their wedding days. Quilts symbolize the heritage of home passed on, the fabric and threads of one life continuing into the next.

Sometimes we dream of how we want our family quilt to look. We choose certain colors or patterns or thread and start to work. We know we want it to be something unique and wonderful. But somehow life shuffles everything around. We lose this but find that. One piece doesn't fit, so another takes its place. The threads get tangled and we have to snip and start over or work the tangles into the design. The quilt we envisioned is not the quilt we hold in our lap. It's turning out differently. The miraculous thing about being a family is that in the last analysis, we are each dependent on one another and God, woven together by mercy given and mercy received.

Sometimes family seems more like a crazy quilt than a carefully designed patchwork. We learn to love each other better through the crises that shape our lives. Through the odd bits and pieces of my own life I've learned a few truths that I've stitched into my crazy quilt, truths like: The appropriate temperature in a home is maintained by warm hearts, not hot heads. A grudge is much too heavy a load for anyone to carry.

The Amish always work a "mistake" into each quilt as a symbol that nothing is perfect. It's a grand idea that comes from living simply and close to the earth. And their quilts are some of the most highly prized throughout the world. Each one is different. Each one is valuable.

Perhaps if we are capable of creating the warm refuge of a family quilt, we may also have the stuff to spin a cocoon and then make a butterfly. While waiting for heaven, let's keep putting those pieces together, stitching them carefully with love and kindness into a patchwork that only we can make.

UPLIFTER

But seek first his kingdom and his righteousness, and all these things will be given to you as well.

MATTHEW 6:33

WAY TO PRAY

Dear Lord, thank You for the quilt of my family. With all its contrasting patterns and frayed edges, as well as its joyful colors, it is the most beautiful thing I've ever seen. I'm so glad for each person You've given me. Thank You that we belong together. Please bless us, Lord, everyone. Amen.

SPREAD YOUR JOY

Your face is a billboard advertising your philosophy of life!

L ord, make me a nail upon the wall. . . ." That's the way one woman's prayer began. A nail. Common and small. "From this," she continued, "hang a bright picture of Thy face." She prayed that others might see Jesus in her.

Recently while traveling to Yucaipa, California, to speak at a women's retreat, I began complaining about how tired I was of sharing my story. My friend Lynda listened as I spoke about how difficult it was to tell the same story, the same gruesome details, over and over: the death of two of my sons, the third son's disappearance into homosexuality, my husband's terrible accident. I didn't feel like spreading any joy that day, because I didn't think I had any to spare. I felt burned-out, exhausted, and empty.

Just then a huge billboard zoomed up out of nowhere, standing beside the highway. In letters ten feet tall were the words "Spread Your Joy," an advertisement for a local church. Like a bolt of lightning, its message struck me to the core. I hadn't wanted to tell my story one more time, to share the joy I found learning to accept life no matter what. Was it just a quirk that the sign appeared at that exact time and place on the highway to Yucaipa, of all places? Was God encouraging me to be faithful?

Lynda burst out laughing. Surely God had overheard our conversation! The conference turned out to be fabulous; I'd rate the results at 110 percent! My energy was high and there was joy in abundance. Many women came forward for prayer; some even gave their lives to Christ for the first time. In sharing my life and the joy God placed deep within (so deep I barely knew where it was anymore), God had restored my own joy.

By choosing to get up on a platform and do what God had called me to do, I was acting as a nail upon the wall of the kingdom of heaven. My story is such a small and insignificant thing compared with many other stories of faith and the story of Jesus Himself. But I chose to stay securely fastened on His wall, holding His picture in place. And you can, too.

Don't get me wrong. I don't usually get billboard messages from God. He doesn't often interrupt my whining with a giant highway sign! He doesn't zoom in on me with a telephoto lens when I feel tired and beat. Life is mostly just getting in the car or on another airplane, climbing the steps to one platform at a time, and faithfully holding His picture in place—whether I feel like it or not. But there is the secret! As we do the thing in front of us, joy comes. It multiplies and eventually hits us smack between the eyes, like a boomerang. It becomes a "hallelujah" in the choir loft of our mind. Joy is a treasure that multiplies by division.

Don't ever abdicate God's call on your life. Too often we expect someone else to fill in for us. We're too tired, too old, too busy. Someone else can fill our shoes, we say. Someone else can do the job. Truth be told, someone else has been relied on far too long, for far too much. It's time we stood up and helped shoulder the burden. Give your gifts, your story, your fortune. Turn the basket upside down and shake every crumb loose. Pour out the vessel. Dump the bucket. Empty your pockets. Tomorrow or the next day or the next you'll have more than ever! Don't give up. Spread your joy!

UPLIFTER

. . . being confident of this, that he who began a good work in you will carry it on to completion until the day of Christ Jesus.
PHILIPPIANS 1:6

WAY TO PRAY

Lord, on my darkest days help me not to give up or hang back. People are waiting to see Your face, to know Your faithfulness, to experience Your joy. Make me a nail for Your picture fastened in place. I surrender my reluctance, even my unbelief. Help me to spread joy! Amen.

THE LITTLEST BOOMERANGS

Sometimes one little spark of kindness is all it takes to reignite the light of hope in a heart that's blinded by pain.

Thousands of women were streaming into the city's convention center for the Friday-night start of the Joyful Journey weekend. They were packing themselves into the already crowded corridors that encircled the arena. It was unusual for the speakers' book tables to be set up in those busy walkways, but in that building there was no other space.

You might think it would have been good for business to have everyone pass by our tables right as the conference began, but buying books was the last thing on those women's minds at that moment. They wanted to find their seats and settle in before the lights were dimmed and the opening session began. To say it was a madhouse doesn't even begin to describe the chaos of the slowly moving throng. The crowds formed a churning, rolling river of faces, all seemingly focused on the seating-section signs over the doorways leading into the auditorium.

At my book table, my daughter-in-love, Shannon, and two other friends were passing out the little flat iridescent marbles I call splashes of joy, along with a card explaining that they're a reminder of God's blessings even in misfortune. Shannon was smiling her widest smile and calling to no one in particular, "Would you like a free splash of joy?" Most women said, "Thanks!" and accepted one without even slowing down.

Then Shannon saw a long line of women, all holding hands, snaking in and out, working its way through the crowd in a slow-motion game of crack the whip. As this chain wove past the book table, Shannon called, "Do you need a splash of joy?"

Only one woman heard. Her head snapped up as though she had been called by name. Without breaking her shuffling gait or changing the focused expression on her face, she released the chain with one hand, extended her palm toward Shannon just long enough to accept the marble, and then regrasped the next hand to keep moving.

The next day a woman from the chain came back to the book table and asked Shannon for one of the marbles. But by that time they had all been given away. "Oh, that's all right," the woman said when Shannon apologized. "Only one member of our group got one, but somehow God made sure it was the person who really needed it."

"What do you mean?" Shannon asked.

"While still on the bus, we agreed to hold hands and snake our way through the auditorium so none of us would get lost in the shuffle. Not one in our group of about thirty even noticed the book table. We didn't hear anyone say anything about a splash of joy. But when we got settled in our seats, the youngest woman in our group, a sweetheart named Sharon, opened her hand and showed us the little shining stone. She said she thought someone called her name, then asked, 'Do you need a splash of joy?' The marble was pressed into her hand. For a while Sharon was convinced it had been given to her by an angel."

Shannon laughed, delighted to have been mistaken for an angel.

The woman continued. "The amazing thing is that of all the women who came, Sharon is the one who is really hurting. Her heart is broken. She's become almost a recluse lately—in fact, this is her first trip away from home since her baby died a few weeks ago. We all prayed something would happen here to ease her pain, and somehow that little splash of joy has been like a spiritual vitamin for her. She laughed for the first time in ages, and we can see she has hope again. That little marble has been a blessing for all of us."

As the woman turned and headed away again, the blessing of that marble boomeranged back to Shannon. And when she shared this story with me, it boomeranged in my direction, too.

UPLIFTER

Now faith is being . . . certain of what we do not see.
HEBREWS 11:1

WAY TO PRAY

Lord, nothing can separate me from You. In fact, sometimes when I experience loss, I can actually see You more clearly. I love You and plan to stay close to Your side. Keep me living in such a way that I can receive your splashes of joy in faith. Amen.

SPREAD HIS LOVE

How can eating a two-pound box of candy possibly make you gain five pounds? It's one of life's great mysteries!

When John Harrison wakes up each Monday morning, he can't wait to get to work by seven-thirty a.m. At age fifty-five, he isn't opting for early retirement. Harrison is the official taste tester for Dreyer's and Edy's Grand ice creams, in the business fifteen years. In fact, he created the first batch of cookies 'n cream flavored ice cream and works on developing new flavors. An ice cream lover from way back—his great-grandfather opened two parlors in New York—Harrison doesn't swallow the stuff at work but puts away about a quart a week at home. "Who'd trust a skinny ice cream taster?" he asks.

Harrison says taste buds (his are insured for a million dollars!) are at their peak early in the day. He'll sample sixty packages of ice cream a day—three hundred a week—concentrating on body and texture as well as the right balance of cream, sweeteners, and flavor. "Smooth and creamy" is what he is tasting for.

"Smooth and creamy?" That's what we all want, isn't it? A job like Harrison's—creative and full of perks. We want to be valued, to become an expert on everything that's sweet and flavorful. Harrison says he never swallows on the job. Once you get full, he claims, you lose the sharpness for tasting subtle nuances and detecting delicate aromas.

Isn't this true of life? The more we stuff ourselves with material pleasures, the less we seem to appreciate life. Don't you know people who have it all—everything but joy, that is? And don't you know people who have very little, who have suffered financial difficulties, family turmoil, and physical problems, and yet bubble with thankfulness and love? Those who have had to wait and work for happiness seem to enjoy it more, because they never take it for granted.

Do you taste life, savoring all the fullness of its flavor? Like Harrison, I wouldn't mind becoming spiritually chubby if it meant I were a living example of someone enjoying the Lord, living off His promises, and bringing the flavor of Jesus Christ to the world. Of course, I would remember not to swallow too much too fast, always with my mind on the goal: glory to God and good stuff for others through my work on earth.

We can't guarantee "smooth and creamy" for ourselves or anybody else. We can never untangle all the woes in other people's lives. We can't produce miracles overnight. But we can bring a cup of cool water to a thirsty soul, or a scoop of laughter to a lonely heart. By being flavorful ourselves, we bring the taste of better things to come so others can take heart.

On a talk show discussing random acts of kindness, one woman told how she walked into an ice cream parlor and paid for the order of the woman in line behind her. What the first woman didn't know was that the second woman was bringing a treat home for a bedridden husband dying of cancer. This simple act of kindness moved the second woman to tears.

If only we were aware of the hope generated by living acts of joy and generosity, we might do many more of them. When we give comfort and relief, remove fears, help carry the burden of someone else, the joy comes back to us as well.

The boomerang power of giving happens *in* us at the very moment we enter the life of someone else in a positive, life-bringing way. Our spirit is lifted, our character is made stronger, our own path is straightened. We become more tolerant and compassionate, flexible and soft. Rough edges are rubbed off, and we get closer to "smooth and creamy." Whenever we do something good for someone else, we are skimming cream from the milk of life.

So go ahead, joke with clerks in ice cream stores and buy an occasional triple-scoop cone for someone next to you in line. Show enthusiasm for your neighbor's children. Tell a family member or friend, "I love you." See beauty in an old and haggard face. Listen to a little child. Pardon the short-comings of a rude stranger. Ignore the grumbling of a grumpy spouse. Find the diamond in the rough.

When things seem hopeless, remember: the Bible says, "And it came to pass . . ." (not "It came to stay")! Once in a while, think of John Harrison and pick up a pint of Dreyer's or Edy's Grand. Someone packed a lot of joy into making that for you. Let it remind you to do the same for others.

UPLIFTER

You will go out in joy and be led forth in peace; the mountains and hills will burst into song before you, and all the trees of the field will clap their hands.

ISAIAH 55:12

WAY TO PRAY

Thank You, heavenly Father, for giving me the senses to taste and enjoy this life on planet Earth. Please make me sensitive to others who haven't as much as I or who have lost their joy for whatever reason. Forgive me for keeping You all to myself. Let me spread Your love. Amen.

GRIPPING HIS GRACE

I've used up all my sick days, so I'm calling in dead.

Mother always told me there would be days like this! We all know we have to go through trials and difficulties. We just don't expect it to be as bad as what Peace Corps volunteers face in the Amazon basin! The U.S. government manual for volunteers sheds some light on what it feels like to live in the real world. In case of attack by an anaconda (weighing up to four hundred pounds and measuring up to thirty-five feet long), it offers the first rule of thumb: "Don't run; the snake is faster than you are." Isn't that just like our troubles? They outweigh us and can outrun us every time.

The manual offers further step-by-step instructions, useful for any of us facing a dilemma in our lives: "Lie flat on the ground, arms by your side and legs together. Tuck your chin in as the anaconda begins to nudge your body. *Do not panic.* Permit it to swallow your feet and ankles." (I'm not making this up; this is coming from the government, folks.) "As the snake sucks your legs into its mouth, be completely still; this will take a long time. When the snake has reached your knees, slowly and with as little movement as possible, reach down to your pocketknife. When the snake reaches your thighs, very gently slide your knife into the side of its mouth, then suddenly rip upward, severing its head." (Second rule of thumb: Be sure to have your knife!)

In this scary world we'd best remember to slow down, lie still, and not panic—and always have our knife! No, Mother didn't tell me it would be this bad. But I'm awfully glad to have learned that God gave us a secret weapon. He always provides a way out of danger, even when we are only fighting our own fears.

Grace is the way out. It's a knife so sharp, the Enemy won't know what hit him. If you feel you are being swallowed whole by your troubles, it's time to grip God's grace. Grace for holding on. Grace for letting go. Grace to be strong. Grace to be weak. Grace to be a warrior. Grace to be a princess. Grace that comes one moment at a time.

Grace is something you need when you buy a suit with an extra pair of matching pants and then proceed to burn a hole in the coat. You need it when, in middle age, your broad mind and narrow waist change places. And then again when a grown child replies, "What do you mean we don't communicate? Just yesterday I faxed you a reply to the message you left on my answering machine!" Take hold of grace and remember that nothing lasts forever, not even your troubles.

One woman asked for prayer from her Bible study group because her husband would not pick up his socks. The lady next to her responded with an incredulous look, saying, "I have a bad heart, a retarded son, and an alcoholic husband given to sporadic violence. An employee my husband fired

McPherson

"OK, YOU'RE DOING GOOD. NOW, ONCE THE
SNAKE REACHES YOUR WAIST, REACH INTO
YOUR POCKET AND GET YOUR KNIFE....
WAIT! DID I SAY WAIST?! I MEANT KNEES!
ONCE THE SNAKE REACHES YOUR KNEES!"

threw a Molotov cocktail into a warehouse we had just filled with stock purchased on credit. It caused the second largest fire our city ever had. We had no insurance. After three years of struggling to pay off the debt, recession forced us into bankruptcy. Would you like to trade places with me?"

Apologizing later, the second lady gripped grace when she told the first lady, "I know playing 'Can you top this?' gives the Lord no glory—and besides, you had all you could handle with the sock problem!" She added, "I've learned a lot over the years. Usually too late."

Somehow, some way, God gives grace to live with a bedroomful of dirty socks, a life littered with broken dreams, or a jungle filled with anacondas. We all have a different story to tell and live out. Be thankful even for your problems; if they were less difficult, someone with less ability might have your job! One of the best results of gripping grace in our own lives is that it produces in us a more gracious, less judgmental response.

Jesus said, "Don't condemn those who are down . . . that hardness can boomerang!" (Luke 6:37, *The Message*). Yep, folks, there is a negative kind of boomerang, too. And believe me, you don't want it. Don't heap heavy burdens on people's backs. Be wise but innocent. Discerning but simple. Whatever you do in your relationships and circumstances, grip His grace.

The mother who says, "Before I was married, I had six theories about bringing up children; now I have six children and no theories" is gripping grace. The zebra who, watching his stripes unravel, says, "I think I'm having stress" needs to grip grace. The guy who wrote the song "I'm Just a Bug on the Windshield of Life" needs badly to grip grace.

Although problems are transitory, our need for grace is not. Gripping grace takes courage, calm, and a will to go on living, to go on loving, to make the best of what we have—or don't have. Thank goodness, grace is our heritage in the Lord Jesus Christ. Grip it, whatever the pickle (or the anaconda!).

UPLIFTER

He mocks proud mockers but gives grace to the humble.
PROVERBS 3:34

WAY TO PRAY

Lord, over and over I have seen You work in my life. It is Your sweet, pure grace regardless of how I mess things up or fail. Your grace redeems the bad days and gives me energy to walk into the good days. Your grace is full of love. Thank You. Amen.

THE GOD OF CHANGE

Change is inevitable, except from a vending machine.

Whenever stress increases, things change, or I feel I am about to blow a gasket, I like to repeat the Serenity Prayer, expanded version. It goes like this:

> God grant me (not my mother-in-law, my child, the neighbor, or the dog) the serenity (that quiet inner calm) to accept (not manipulate or tolerate) the things I cannot change (as much as I would like to), the courage (action in the face of fear) to change the things I can (people aren't things—I need to keep telling myself), and the wisdom (knowing without necessarily knowing how I know) to know the difference (like when to mind my own business). Amen.

Like it or not, constant change is part of modern life. And much as I consider myself a woman of the nineties, I can become sentimental at times. It happened recently at an estate sale. I arrived early, wandering through rooms in the old house, feeling as though the family might round the corner any moment. The china was still stacked in cupboards, the knickknacks still on the shelves. The beds were made and extra linens were carefully folded into open dresser drawers. In the living room, beside the television, lay a stack of newspapers; peeking out between them was a child's drawing, scribbled with the greeting "From Josh, For Grandpa." My eyes welled up. I could see Josh playing on the floor, the old couple still sitting on the sofa.

More shoppers arrived and started poking through the house. People my age often joke with their kids about selling off stuff when they are dead and gone. But that day it didn't seem funny. I left the sale without buying a thing and started thinking about what in the world *doesn't* change. I made a list.

1. God's love.
2. Friendship with His son.
3. The power of the Holy Spirit.

That's about as far as I got. And that's about as far as I needed to go.

When you think you've had just about all the change you can stand, reach out and take one step further into God's wide arms. Though His love, friendship, and power never change, He made you with a big elastic spiritual cord that stretches with every tug and pull. He knows exactly how much *give* it's got. If He's calling you to stretch, He knows you've got what it takes. Reach! You'll become more confident and enthusiastic about life if you do. You'll discover that serenity comes not just from peaceful days and stable routines but in flux, in motion, in the midst of an adventure when you stretch beyond your comfort zone.

It's always a challenge to talk about the odd turns and twists in my life in a way that will redeem and uplift people.

Shortly after my book *Splashes of Joy in the Cesspools of Life* came out, I was invited to a megachurch in Arizona. Speaking about cesspools, as you might imagine, is not a pretty job. But when I walked into the banquet room in Arizona that day, I was shocked and delighted by what I saw.

Rolls of pink, yellow, blue, and white toilet tissue had been gracefully draped all around the room. Streamers formed a wistful curtain to hide the edge of the speaker's platform. On the platform were three complete toilets covered with gold paper and sparkly stuff! Each of the fifty tables was set with a rubber plunger centerpiece covered with pink feathers, white pearls, and toilet tissue bows. When the meeting started, the director of women's ministry stood up and said, "Let's plunge right in, ladies!" then taught us a little song to the tune of "Jingle Bell Rock": "Flush away, flush away, flush away all . . ."

After an hour or two of singing, swinging, swaying, and me speaking, I was presented with a farewell gift—a toilet seat encrusted with pearls and trimmed with feathers, sprayed all over with more sparklies. My husband, Bill, carried it all the way back to California, and you'd better believe he was the talk of the airport!

I was reminded once again that we can take distasteful things and turn them into something true and beautiful. That's what God does! He knows change can make your life *richer*. If you find your current change distressful, encrust it with sequins and feathers, wrap it in gold foil paper, receive it as a gift with delight and appreciation. Live for today but hold your hands open to tomorrow. Anticipate the future and its changes with joy. There is a seed of God's love in every event, every circumstance, every unpleasant situation in which you may find yourself. Don't get stuck in a rut or hung up on an outdated blessing. You serve a God of change!

UPLIFTER

Do not store up for yourselves treasures on earth, where moth and rust destroy, and where thieves break in and steal. But store up for yourselves treasures in heaven.... For where your treasure is, there your heart will be also.

MATTHEW 6:19–21

WAY TO PRAY

Lord, whatever comes, let me respond with my own "Whatever, Lord!" In everything, I'm seeking treasure of the spirit, letting go of yesterday and reaching for tomorrow. Grant me serenity through all the ups and downs. Amen.

JOY—A BOOMERANG WEAPON

If at first you don't succeed, skydiving is not for you.

Some people can do just about anything well. And some people have a tough time doing just about anything at all. I thought I was one of the former, until my granddaughters began to tell me about all the wonderful technological advances I've missed. The truth is, prepaid phone cards arrived on the scene just when I'd finally memorized the number on my old-fashioned calling card. Computer programs that can design just about any kind of sane or insane letter imaginable confound me. I still rely on my faithful IBM Selectric typewriter to write my books. After all, Erma Bombeck typed hers on the same kind of machine, and if it was good enough for Erma, it's good enough for me! To make matters worse, I still mimeograph my newsletters, and I've never once spotted the entry ramp to that information superhighway called the Internet.

There is an Internet address, I'm told, that tutors you in all the life skills your parents didn't teach you, things like opening a coconut, changing the oil in your car, coping with insomnia, or shaving your legs smoothly. Now if I only had step-by-step instructions on how to get into the Internet!

I may not be among those who succeed the first time (or anytime soon). But the trouble with doing something right the first time is that nobody will be able to appreciate how difficult it was to do in the first place. What I am good at is trying again and again.

One thing I have succeeded in is knowing how to do goofy things regularly as a treat for myself. I believe in having fun, because I know that *she who laughs, lasts.* A lady named Eleanor Whitesides once wrote, "My friend, you wore your Jesus like an iron-on patch. But He could not cover the holes in your shabby coat. Yet when you laid aside that threadbare rag and laughed with me, and wept with me, and simply loved me, I saw His love in you. And you wore a shining robe which drew me to His side."

Recently a super-special dad had been having some super-special problems and sensed his family needed a lift. He said to me, "What we really need is a visitation from the angels!"

So the next day Marilyn (my partner in fun and crime) and I went off to a nearby church, where we slipped into the baptismal room unnoticed and swiped (I mean borrowed) two long, full, flowing baptismal gowns. Then we drove over near our friend's house and donned the gowns. The mailman nearly dropped his pouch when he saw two women get out of a car with "SPATULA" on the license plates, toss on white robes with heavy weights in the bottom, and go clinking down the street. Several houses later we appeared at the door as the angel messengers so desperately needed by our friend and his dear family. I was thinking how wonderful it is that God gives us robes of righteousness to clink around in. If we get them dirty or drag them in the dirt, He has instant detergent, cleaning them daily from the grime we walk through.

Some people say, "When you do a good deed, get a receipt, in case heaven is like the IRS." We didn't get a receipt that day, except the beautiful feeling we carried home with us.

Whatever you do, whether it's impersonating angels, jumping from airplanes, visiting the sick, surfing the Net, taking care of widows, or goofing off, do it well and never lose your ability to scatter joy. Tuck some in the pocket of the stranger next to you at the grocery store. Sprinkle it on the head of an elderly lady crossing the street in front of you. Leave funny messages in your teenagers' cars or on their E-mail. Wake up your spouse with the scent of roses or honeysuckle. And never ever forget to smile.

Smiles are like two-for-one coupons. Each time you let them spread across your lips, they light up the face and heart of someone else. Sooner or later a smile will come back around to you just when you need it most. Talk about a win-win situation; move over, Stephen Covey!

Joy is the ultimate boomerang weapon. And it is something anyone—everyone—can do well.

UPLIFTER

For nothing is impossible with God.

LUKE 1:37

WAY TO PRAY

Lord, help me do something worthwhile for someone else today. I want to bring a smile to the face of my neighbor. Love a friend through me and help me succeed in bringing joy to his or her life. Amen.

NO PERFECT PEOPLE

Have we forgotten that we're all born the same way:
naked, wet, and hungry? Then things get worse!

I'm used to getting calls from mothers who've gone completely bananas. I've been there myself, in the states of *losing it* and *lost it*. You reach a point when you no longer try to keep it all "together." It starts with failing to wipe away the fingerprints on the walls and ends whenever, with whatever crises occur. As things veer out of control, you find yourself asking, "Who stopped payment on my reality check?"

Christians sometimes have more trouble handling trouble than the world does, because we think we should be perfect. Not so. We're just forgiven and, I hope, forgiving. Too often, though, our faith is shallow. We cling to the padded cross instead of the "old rugged" cross of the hymn. What should set us apart is our trust, our ability to let God loose in our circumstances rather than forever trying to control them ourselves.

Admit it and save yourself years of worry. There are no superfamilies. There are no perfect people. Striving for constant protection is like playing leapfrog with a unicorn. Ouch! At some point (excuse the pun) you have to let go and let God be God. Such surrender usually happens by degrees, of course. But it does happen—and what tremendous freedom results!

I received a letter once from a mother who has experienced this freedom. Listen to her story.

I got so weary after two years of waking up at two a.m. with pains in my stomach. I knew if I kept it up, I would be completely ruined. So I "had it out" with God. I pointed out to Him that my daughter is His more than she is mine and that He loves her more than I do. I said, "God, You take care of her. You know how to reach her where I cannot." At that time I laid down my burden and left it!

I no longer have any guilt, for I know I was the best mother I knew how to be. I probably made lots of mistakes, but no one could ever say I didn't care.... [Acknowledging this] has worked to get me through this terrible depression of knowing my daughter was a lesbian. Perhaps my story will help some other mother who is where I was a year ago.

Parents have all sorts of emotional responses when they learn a child is homosexual. If you read my book, you know I suffered from "itchy teeth." One mother lost all her hair within a week of learning her son was gay. When I met her, she pulled her scarf from her head to reveal only some fine downy patches of hair, like on a hamster. I felt relieved when she covered up her scalp again with her scarf.

Sometime later the phone rang and a cheery voice said, "Remember the lady with the hamster hair?" How could I forget? "Well," she continued, "I wanted you to know that my hair has grown out full and thick, and today I got myself an afro!"

How awesome to know that hair can grow out, stomach pains stop, and teeth quit itching! Hearts can be mended, too, though it takes a little longer. Part of that process is learning to live with heartache, because results don't usually materialize right away.

One father wrote,

If I were asked by an unseen voice to name the one quality I would like to pass on to my son, I would say, "Help him, O Lord, to take whatever life brings." For this, more than any quality in life, is the one which counts and by which men and women are finally counted.

You are right where X marks the spot on the map of life. Whatever dilemma you're facing, ask yourself what difference it will make one hundred years from today. The difference is in letting go and letting God. He'll never let you down. I've received calls and letters from moms who've gone bananas; I've received just as many from mothers who've learned the secret of surrender. They know God is to be trusted—even with our children. He'll help us face tomorrow with open hands, open heart, open mind, and tons o' confidence.

After I hung up the phone following my conversation with my friend with the hamster hair, I thanked God that her afro is a sign of His faithfulness and of restoration and new growth. Take heart! Take courage! Count your blessings, not your losses. And thank God that although you may show other symptoms of total panic, at least you've never had hamster hair, have you?

UPLIFTER

"No weapon forged against you will prevail.... This is the heritage of the servants of the LORD, and this is their vindication from me," declares the LORD.

ISAIAH 54:17

WAY TO PRAY

Thank You, Lord, for my children and all the memories I have raising them. I am doing the best I can in the job You gave me. Whatever problems arise, help me to remember that I am equal to the task, because every trial is filtered through Your hands. I trust You, for I know You love my children so much more than I do. And that's a lot! Amen.

"IN THE 42 YEARS WE WERE TOGETHER FRANK NEVER REALLY LET GO OF HIS NAVY DAYS."

LIFE IS LOOKING UP

Time is the best teacher; unfortunately, it kills all its students.

How often have you heard that Christians are not settlers here on earth but pilgrims? Do you really believe it? And if you are interested in the hereafter, do you realize that the *here* always determines the *after?* Live for Jesus now, I always say, and spend eternity in the nonsmoking section!

Here's another one-liner: "Life is hard and then you die." Does that sound discouraging? Actually, it's the strongest message of encouragement I know, because we have not even begun to taste the glory, love, grace, and joy that God intends for us! A friend sent me a darling card with a picture of a fabulous home on the front. Inside she wrote, "This is the mansion I have ordered for heaven. And I hope yours is next to mine." I framed that picture and now it hangs in my joy room, daily reminding me that heaven's lavish mansions will have no dead-bolt locks, window guards, or burglar alarms.

Heaven is a protected place prepared for the poor in spirit (Matt. 5:3). Perhaps you have already made, as I have, some deposits there: friends and family members who've gone before you. You'll get them back with interest! Imagine stepping into heaven and grasping hold of hands held out to steady yours, the hands of God Himself. Then other hands will reach out to welcome you. Familiar faces will crowd your homecoming. You will pass from tempest to calm, feeling invigorated by immortality. A lady wrote to me that she wanted this on her tombstone: "Don't cry for me; I'm finally where I wanna be!"

Someone has said that in heaven you'll never again turn on a light switch (Rev. 21:23, 25), lock a door (Rev. 21:25, 27), dry tears from your cheeks (Rev. 21:4), take Advil (Rev. 21:4), or drive by a hospital or a cemetery (Rev. 21:4). Meanwhile remember that each day is a gift from God; that's why it's called the present. And each dark night is like secret buried treasure because you can learn lessons at night that you might never have recognized by day. And while you're learning, humor can ease the pain.

"One of the things I like about laughter is that it cannot be buried; it lives on," says George Goldtrap. He then recounts the story of a preacher conducting his first funeral, who pointed to the body and as solemnly as he knew how, declared, "What we have here is only a shell. The nut is already gone—to heaven!" Then there's the one about the hypochondriac whose tombstone read, "Now do you believe me when I told you I was sick?" Mel Blanc, the voice of Daffy Duck and Porky Pig cartoons, wanted his epitaph to read: "Th-Th-Th-That's all, folks!"

Bottom line: every calendar should carry a warning similar to the one on automobile side mirrors: "Warning: dates on calendar are closer than they appear." You never know when your time is going to expire, so remember: as you add years to your life, it is more important to add life to your years.

So how will you use the years God gives you? Experts say the average person will spend six years eating, five years waiting in lines, four years doing housework, three years attending meetings, two years playing telephone tag, one year searching for lost items, and six months sitting at red lights. How will you use those moments and hours?

Will you be remembered for being a fault finder? Or will you be known for your quick smile, the laugh lines around your eyes, and the twinkle deep within? After all, the Lord gives you your face, but you provide the expression! Will you be known for puritanical attitudes (the haunting fear that someone, somewhere, may be happy!) or for the slight stoop of the shoulders gained from reaching over to help friends who have fallen?

It's never too late to change your attitude as you prepare to change altitude. Attitude is the mind's paintbrush; it can color any situation. For every minute you are angry, sad, or anxious, you lose sixty entire seconds of happiness. Between yesterday's regret and tomorrow's dream lies today's opportunity. Use it.

Did you hear the story of the two frogs that fell into a bucket of cream? They tried to get out by climbing up the side of the bucket but each time slipped back down. Finally one frog said, "I give up!" and he drowned. The other decided he had nothing to lose by keeping at it. Lo and behold, he found that all his kicking churned up a lump of butter, and leaping on top of the lump, he hopped out! Enthusiasm set him free! Make enthusiasm your daily habit while waiting and working for the kingdom of God. Don't get hung up on the very bad—or the very good—on this earth.

Some years back I received an exciting phone call from a man in Canada inviting me to speak to career women in Vancouver and then take a cruise and have tea with the queen.

"What queen?" I asked.

"Why, the queen of England," he said.

After I explained that I didn't charge a set fee but accepted whatever honorarium was given, he proceeded to tell me that if I would come to speak, go on the cruise, and have tea with the Queen, he would pay me fifty thousand dollars! Bill was sitting next to me and overheard the conversation. His immediate response was, "Ask him if he means Canadian money or American?" Bill just wanted the facts!

In the end the queen didn't come that year because of family problems. But when I told my darling daughter-in-love, Shannon, about the invitation, she responded, "Well, it is wonderful that the queen is coming, but I would really rejoice if it were the King!"

Time is short. Live your life looking up. When our King comes to redeem His own, what a day of rejoicing that will be. Get ready for the royal treatment; let Jesus be King of your life!

UPLIFTER

Teach us to number our days aright, that we may gain a heart of wisdom.

PSALM 90:12

WAY TO PRAY

Heavenly Father, bless this humble dwelling You've given me in which to live this life on earth. You are the rock of my life. You are my strong tower. Nothing on this earth is worth the time I spend worrying about it. One day at Your feet in heaven will be worth it all. Help me to look up and remember that a time is coming when I will step ashore and find I've come home! Amen.

DON'T PARK THERE!

Never let your burdens paralyze your progress.

One day I parked my car where I wasn't supposed to. As I got out, a loud male voice boomed at me: "Mrs. Spa-toola, you aren't allowed to park there!" (My car carries the license plates "SPATULA," representing the name of our ministry that grew out of my first book, *Where Does a Mother Go to Resign?*) As I climbed back into the car, I remembered a sign I once saw that said, "Don't even *think* of parking here!" How many of us, I began to wonder, park in life's no-parking zones?

As believers in God almighty, there are places where we should definitely not, under any circumstances, even *think* of parking.

Do not park by life's defeats. This is the biggest of those places. Where has life beaten you? Got you down? You feel ashamed, humiliated, tainted. Don't park there! Move on.

Do not park at anger. Not even anger at yourself. Flailing at God or anyone else is a normal emotional feeling unrelated to who you are spiritually. At times anger is appropriate, but don't get stuck in it. In order to move on, you may have to find ways to ventilate so you can begin to heal. Storing up

GET EVEN WITH GUESTS WHO SNOOP IN YOUR MEDICINE CABINET. FILL IT WITH MARBLES BEFORE YOUR NEXT PARTY.

hostility will only boomerang on you in the long run. Things hurt. As Colin Powell says, "Get mad, then get over it."

Do not park at escape. There is no good time for quitting. If your child avoids you, don't give up; find a kid and hug him. If your spouse forgets you, send *him* flowers. If your friend fails to call, pick up the phone yourself. Keep sowing fun and sunshine in your life, planting seeds of love. Don't give up, get going!

Do not park at discouragement. If you're not a natural optimist, you can develop the ability to see the lighter side of things. Colin Powell also says, "Perpetual optimism is a force multiplier, a way of increasing your forces." (And your focus!) Optimism actually promotes physical as well as emotional healing. If you're traveling back from the pit of despair, put one foot in front of the other and head toward the light.

I once got a phone call from a gal who said her name was Mary Hart, and she wanted information about our ministry. I took her address and she spelled her name for me: M-e-r-r-y H-e-a-r-t. I said, "How darling! I hope you don't go and marry someone with a dumb name and ruin it." She told me she was in fact engaged—to a man named Hogaboom! (Maybe he should change his name to hers, eh?)

Do not park at any particular age. Some people say life begins at forty—to disintegrate, that is! So what if you're getting older. We all are and the neat thing is, it isn't our fault! No blame game here. Too bad you can't do as many cartwheels as you could when you were a kid. But you can still be inquisitive, flexible, impulsive, and adventurous. No hardening of the attitudes allowed. Hang loose. Go with the flow.

Do not park at worry. Erma Bombeck asked, "Is worry a curse—or is it a virtue that elevates us to the highest form of life?" We can't push a magic button to make worrisome thoughts go away. But we can discipline our minds to think on what is right and true and lovely (Phil. 4:8). Remembering this is like taking off the hand brake and moving ahead. Who knows what possibilities we will encounter just around the corner? Jesus promised that our Father knows our every need and will not fail to provide (Matt. 6:31–33).

Do not park at guilt. Move on by receiving Jesus as your Savior, accepting God's forgiveness, and freely forgiving others. Put the past behind you. Begin again. On the journey learn all you can from your mistakes, and with God's help make a U-turn at each one.

Recently I spoke at a conference located in a remote area of Nebraska. My cabin was perched just above a train trestle. By day the railroad tracks I saw from my window shone with an almost radiant brightness as the sun moved toward the horizon. The highly polished rails gleamed against the ties and ballast like glowing ribbons of steel. Each night I listened carefully for the first far-off toots of the horn, then pictured the train passing and racing on into the night. Before long I could distinguish one kind of locomotive from another by the notes of the air horn and the drumming of the engines.

With trains rumbling by almost hourly, some women complained that the noise kept them awake all night. But I was fascinated. The sound reminded me of faraway times and places and that we are all on our way somewhere. Trains keep moving on, going about their business, doing the work of conveying people and products to important places. They never park; they pause just long enough to accomplish the purpose of their trip.

I want to be like those trains, with plenty of room for anybody who wants to climb aboard. I don't want to park anywhere on this earth; I want to keep doing what God has called me to do. I hope somebody somewhere will enjoy the sound and be inspired as I clack along my track.

We are all on our way somewhere. We'll get there if we just keep going.

UPLIFTER

Since we are surrounded by such a great cloud of witnesses, let us throw off everything that hinders and the sin that so easily entangles, and let us run with perseverance the race marked out for us. Let us fix our eyes on Jesus.

HEBREWS 12:1–2

WAY TO PRAY

Keep me moving on, Lord. Not parked. Amen.

GOD'S SPIRITUAL STOVE

*Evangelism is no more than one beggar telling
another beggar where he found bread.*

A cold day. It swirls snow, kicking up a storm. Icicles dangle from the nostrils of every rainspout. I breathe arctic vapors, shiver, and blow steam through chapped lips, beating hands together for a smidgen of warmth. Have you noticed in cold climates how people seem to hibernate during the winters? It takes something extra to stick to the job, keep your kids happy in the house, get to church, and be a good neighbor in those frosty winter months.

We experience frigid temperatures in our faith, too. There are cold days when hope dies: love walks out the door, a friend moves out of town, the job ends, the bank fails. God seems distant. Prayer fades in your throat before you barely utter a word. The Bible stares back with a blank page. You might call it spiritual frostbite. It is painful. Poisonous. Dangerous.

The church is God's spiritual stove. In its containment we pile on fuel, stir the embers, strike a match. James indicates that if we say, "Keep warm and well fed" and do nothing tangible for people who are cold and hungry, there is no profit in it (James 2:16). We need each other's warmth to survive the winters of our lives. We need a place to thaw, even a handout sometimes, if only in the form of encouraging words.

Henry Ward Beecher stopped to talk with a newsboy on a blustery morning. "Aren't you cold?" he asked. The boy answered, "I was until you came, sir." To a soul that is starved for human kindness or warmth, even a casual but personal question can be life-giving, because it shows you care.

You are a member of Christ's body, the church. Will you warm someone else today? People who get snowed in while mountain climbing are instructed to build an ice cave, keep their boots on, and lie down next to each other, sharing the heat of their bodies in order to survive. When you warm someone else with a smile, a hug, or pat on the back, you receive their warmth back. We comfort one another "with the comfort we ourselves have received," wrote the apostle Paul (2 Cor. 1:4). "If two lie down together, they will keep warm. But how can one keep warm alone?" said the preacher (Eccl. 4:11).

Stand by someone who is standing alone. A single woman or a lonely teenager out there aches for someone to put an arm around them and squeeze tight. Unless you've been there, you have no idea how good that feels to a person who gets little or no affection. Not everyone has a spouse, parent, or friend who offers physical touch, but everybody needs it. Experts say twelve hugs is the minimum daily requirement.

Someone said, "I know I'm not what I should be and I'm not yet what I'm going to be. But I'm not what I was—I'm on

"THE WEATHERMAN DID SAY THERE
WOULD BE LOCALIZED SNOW SQUALLS."

my way because you touched me." Touch someone with a warm word. There are people who are subject to other people's complaints all day long. Give a compliment or friendly greeting to a store clerk, janitor, nurse, or office manager. Their ears are hungry for something positive, encouraging, and healthful to the spirit. See what a variety of loving phrases you can offer that will bring a smile to the face of people you meet. Challenge yourself! Make a game of it. Just bring joy today.

A little girl was late walking home from school one day, and her mother was angry and worried. The girl explained that her friend had tripped on the sidewalk, stumbled, and broken her doll on the way home. "Well, did you stop to help her fix it?" asked the girl's mother. "Is that why you're late?"

"No, Mommy, we knew we couldn't fix it, but I stopped to help her cry."

In the extreme cold of life we need each other. Don't be fooled by the facade of strength that some put on to protect themselves. Put a little May and June into someone's life. Don't hide behind propriety. As the U.S. Army admonishes, "Be all that you can be." As your kindergarten teacher taught you, "Be a buddy." Look both ways—who needs a hand, a word, or one of your ears for a few moments? Lending yours might mean making someone's day. Reach out and warm a heart!

UPLIFTER

An anxious heart weighs a man down, but a kind word cheers him up.

PROVERBS 12:25

WAY TO PRAY

Lord, someone I'll meet today is lonely or afraid. Give me Your words to bring that person comfort, courage, or calm. Help me warm a friend or stranger who is tired and cold. I want to be a harbinger of spring. Amen.

WATERPROOFING LIFE

~

Jesus didn't say, "Let your light so twinkle."
He said, "Let it so shine!"

Human beings thrive on laughter. Since most of us can't afford vacations in Hawaii, we have to learn to make our own fun! The best way to do that is to keep your state of mind green and golden: find, recycle, or produce joy wherever and however you can. A good humorist is a work of heart! The Hasidic Jews believe that the best way to worship God is by being happy. They incorporate dance and celebration into their spiritual walk.

Today make yourself a joy box and start collecting things that make you smile or laugh. First you'll need a shoe box. Then you might want a basket. Later a barrel. And before you know it, you may have to add a room onto your home, as Bill and I did in order to have a place large enough to hold everything. My joy room has become a haven to many others who just need a place to kick back, put life in neutral, and smile

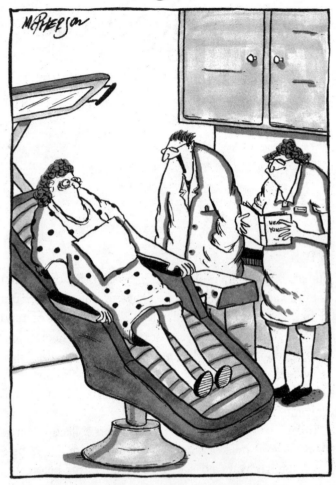

"UNFORTUNATELY, WE'RE ALL OUT OF LAUGHING GAS, SO IN LIEU OF IT, JOYCE IS GOING TO READ HENNY YOUNGMAN JOKES TO YOU THROUGHOUT YOUR ROOT CANAL."

again. Just sitting in there is a form of therapy. Even the clock seems to chime out the message "I love you, friend!"

Having returned at one point in time from the black pit into new life, I feel I have earned this joy room, where the walls are filled with laughter. One of the things I treasure most is a wooden plaque inscribed with the name "Barbara" and its meaning: "Coming with joy" (1 Thess. 3:12). I'll never forget the woman who said to me, "I feel like I'm living in a parenthesis; the horrible parenthesis of life!" I know how she feels. You try to get ahead of that closure, and the way out escapes you. You feel closed-in, trapped in an emotional closet. I've found that "coming with joy" into the lives of people who feel trapped helps free them. Each time someone laughs, the raw edges heal, the rough ache subsides.

Sometimes you have to hunt and peck for things that hit your funny bone. You can even find something to laugh at in the Bible, for the Bible is like the ocean—you can wade in it, feed from it, live on it, or drown in it. Here's what some kids wrote after studying the Bible.

> Noah's wife was called Joan of Ark.
> Moses went to the top of My Cyanide to get the Ten Commandments.
> Joshua led the Hebrews in the battle of Geritol.
> David fought the Finkelsteins, people who lived in biblical times.
> The people who followed Jesus were called the Twelve Decibels.
> The epistles were the wives of the apostles.

Humor is the chocolate chips in the ice cream of life. Remember the old-time "Good Humor man" who drove his ice cream truck down every street in the neighborhood, chiming a jingle on those hot summer days? All the kids came running as soon as they heard the sound. But good humor doesn't drive down many streets anymore. You have to go out and get it. Fortunately, it's not that hard to find.

One woman told about buying a new pair of Gore-tex boots. Wearing them for the first time, she came across a puddle and quickly avoided it. She didn't want to get her brand-new boots muddy. After dodging several puddles, she suddenly realized why she had bought the boots in the first place! The next puddle she came to, she stepped in lightly. The next one she plunged into. The next she leaped into with the enthusiasm of a two-year-old. By the time she got home, her boots were caked with mud, her feet were dry, and her heart was happy.

Humor is the waterproofing of life. With it you can take on all the mud puddles life puts in your way. Don't avoid them, don't step lightly through them. Jump! Splash! Dare them to defeat you. God promises a safe landing, not a calm voyage. He restores to you the joy of your salvation. Nothing, not even the worst sin (or mud!), can separate you from Him.

Remember, when you fall down, you gotta giddy up! Rise to the occasion. And rise early for the sheer joy of it. The Bible says joy comes in the morning (Ps. 30:5). Abraham rose early to stand before the Lord (Gen. 19:27). Jacob rose early to worship the Lord (Gen. 28:18). Moses rose early to meet God on Sinai (Ex. 34:4). Joshua rose early to fight for the Lord (Josh. 6:12; 8:10). Ezekiel rose early to receive the word of the Lord (Ezek. 12:8). Jesus rose early to speak with His Father (Mark 1:35). God's loving kindnesses and compassions "are new every morning" (Lam. 3:22–23).

"Thou shalt not wallow in it," says the *Humor Gazette*. Get up early and get on with life. "He will yet fill your mouth with laughter," says Job (8:21). The psalmist wrote, "My mouth is filled with your praise" (Ps. 71:8). Don't settle for chortles or giggles. Go for the guffaw! Why settle for twinkle when you can shine?

A little boy looked out his window at bedtime and saw the crescent moon. "Look, Daddy," he said. "There's a smile in the sky." Yes, there is! Not only in the moon but in the stars. Jesus is the "morning star" (Rev. 2:28). Someday the trumpet will sound, the dead will rise, and we will be caught up to meet Him in the skies (1 Thess. 4:16–17). If that doesn't make you smile, I don't know what will!

UPLIFTER

In the same way, let your light shine before men, that they may see your good deeds and praise your Father in heaven.

MATTHEW 5:16

WAY TO PRAY

Dear Lord, sometimes it's not much fun here on earth. But I am committed to joy. Full and everlasting joy. Show me how to find it or create it. Show me how to fill the lives of others with the happiness that comes from knowing You. I love You, Lord! Amen.

THE MESSAGES OF HANDS

~e

You can't climb the ladder of life with your hands in your pockets.

Hands are silent couriers carrying messages from our hearts. They open doors to bid you welcome. They push a swing for a laughing youngster. They gently brush away tears of pain. My hand on your shoulder offers compassion. A hand-clasp conveys strength and courage. A wave of the hand says good-bye to a friend or beckons a stranger who is lonely. An infant delightedly curls his dimpled fingers around my wrinkled ones. No words are spoken. None are needed.

We use our hands in so many different ways. Here's the way one missionary woman used hers: first to bake missionary cake, then to write the recipe so *we* might enjoy it.

Prepare fire in mud stove. Rinse utensils with boiled water. Check flour for bugs. Measure and sift flour and sugar. Stop to kill cockroach crawling across the table. Add two eggs. (Oops, none left; have Johnny fetch from tribal neighbors.) While waiting, pull lizard out of grass hut roof and throw outside. Crack eggs. (Uh-oh, they're duck eggs. Use anyway; who's going to know?) Add lemon juice. (No lemons; substitute papaya juice.)

Stir. Put in greased pan and sprinkle with palm nuts. Bake until cake rises. Serves a family of six or a few hungry village children!

ADAPTED FROM MRS. JOY BENZIO, TRANS-WORLD
RADIO HEADQUARTERS

You can do loving things with your own hands today: organize a drawer, pick a bouquet of wildflowers, write in your journal, draw a picture card for a child, pat a puppy, braid a little girl's hair, make a batch of cookies, decorate a wall or a shelf, pinch a cheek, pull some weeds, wash your husband's car. The boomerang joy in all this is that the hand that gives, gathers!

One day I was in a Thrifty Drug store. Because the name of our ministry is Spatula, I am always on the lookout for cheap plastic spatulas to give away. My supply was low and the spatula I had been using at meetings looked more like a kitty litter scooper. That day in Thrifty I saw a salesgirl kneeling down and sorting out a large box of kitchen utensils. Among them were brightly colored plastic spatulas for only fifteen cents apiece! I excitedly asked if I could sort through the utensils with her, picking out all the spatulas. I found about thirty and gleefully loaded them into my shopping cart. "I am so happy," I told the cashier. "Do you have any idea how hard it is to find such *nice* spatulas so *cheap?*"

She shot me a funny look as she swooped up my cartload of spatulas and stuffed them into a sack. I figured it was more fun *not* explaining what I wanted them for.

I took those thirty spatulas and passed them out as a cheerful reminder that we use our hands as well as our hearts when we rescue a friend, sister, or neighbor when she's hit the ceiling and has to be scraped off. In God's big kitchen, these handy utensils can be used for so many things.

Remember, God provides the ingredients for our daily bread but expects us to do the baking. With our own hands!

UPLIFTER

May the favor of the Lord our God rest upon us; establish the work of our hands for us—yes, establish the work of our hands.
PSALM 90:17

WAY TO PRAY

You are almighty God, and yet You allow me to be Your hands and feet on earth. How priceless that You anoint me for ministry using my own two hands. Thank You, Lord. And show me how much I can do with what You've already given me. Amen.

ADVICE FOR THE HUMOR-IMPAIRED

*I still go out frequently. Of course, now
I do it in pieces: my back, my neck, my knees . . .*

They say that once you're old enough to know all the answers, nobody asks you the questions anymore. But TV journalist Dan Rather once asked a 106-year-old man to disclose his secret of long life. The old man rocked back and forth in his chair before answering. Finally he replied, "Keep breathing."

Sure, growing older is stressful—almost as bad as growing *up*—but using your funny bone to subdue that kind of stress works wonders! When you hear *snap, crackle, pop,* and it isn't your cereal—don't panic. Instead let your imagination rather than your blood pressure soar. One study showed that even humor-impaired people can counteract a negative response to stress by rescripting their circumstances in terms of a television sitcom or a comedy movie.

"Coping humor" is an acquired skill that helps distance you from your troubles. Some scientists believe humor provides long-term health benefits and even prolongs life. Laughter defuses insults, soothes aching muscles, and counteracts the humiliation of what is happening to your body and mind.

Developing coping humor is like discovering a freshwater spring on your property. It is a resource from which to continually draw nourishing supplies of life-giving elixir. Strive to be like the woman who, losing her leg in an accident, turned to the doctor and said, "Thank God it was the leg with the arthritis!"

Gerontologist Ann E. Gerike says we can develop a new way of thinking about our physical limitations as we age. After a lifetime of straining to be "the perfect perky ideal," finally your breasts can relax, she encourages. And that extra weight around the middle (hence the term "middle age"?)—it's just cuddlier body lines! So as birthdays come, don't think of yourself as growing old; you've just reached that vibrant metallic age: silver in your hair, gold in your teeth, and lead in your bottom!

Someone once said, "I used to take each day as it came, one at a time. Now I'm down to a half day at a time!" Growing older is sometimes like climbing a steep hill. You can complain, "Too many rocks in the way and bumps on the road!" Or you can look at it this way: "I'd like to live my life in the fast lane, but I'm married to a speed bump." But the most productive way is to put your intellect and spirit to work doing what you do best!

In 1956 Harland Sanders, out of work as a sixty-six-year-old in Corbin, Kentucky, loaded his car with a pressure cooker and a fifty-pound can of his secret blend of eleven herbs and spices. Visiting restaurants, he told the owners, "Let me cook chicken for you. If you like the way it tastes, I'll teach you how to cook it my way and give you a franchise; you pay me a five-cent royalty on every chicken you sell." Sander's idea became the largest and most successful chicken business in the world, and he lived another thirty-three years to enjoy the fruits of his labor! So rise to the occasion when you'd most like to recline in a rocker!

Last winter Bill and I decided to spend our Christmas holidays in Washington state. Because I've never needed a heavy wrap in southern California, Bill went shopping with me to prepare for the trip, and we picked out a lovely black shawl, soft and fuzzy, with fringe decorating the edge. Then Bill gave me a sparkly Christmas tree pin to wear on it. Off we went, me feeling luxurious in my warm new shawl!

That was the year terrible snowstorms hit Seattle. After enjoying a white Christmas, we reached the airport to return to California, only to discover that all the planes had been grounded. No busses or trains were running, either. Thousands of people had to camp out in the airport. Bill and I spent two days sitting and sleeping on the floor, waiting for the storms to subside. The restaurants ran out of food, the bathrooms ran out of soap and paper, and everywhere people ran out of patience. Hungry and grubby, we waited like everyone else for a plane to take us home. We could grumble or we could look for a way to add joy to this challenging experience.

On the third day of this suffering, I became friends with a darling pregnant mother who had been chasing two little kids around. She was exhausted from trying to corral them and keep them happy without enough food or snacks to satisfy them. Finally the kids collapsed to take a nap amid the hassle. Without pillows they looked uncomfortable, so I folded my black shawl to make one, with just enough left over to cover their poor mother's legs. I smiled as they settled down to sleep. Just then I heard my name on the pager system.

Amazingly, the snow had been shoveled just enough to allow one plane to escape, and Bill and I were going to be on it! Prior to boarding, I took one look at that pregnant mother asleep with two kids curled up on my soft, warm shawl. Should I wake them to retrieve it? No way! I wouldn't use it again anyway until the next time I headed to a cold climate. (And at that point I seriously doubted I would live long enough to ever make another airplane trip!) So I grabbed my carry-on and headed for the plane with Bill.

Now whenever I am tempted to miss my fuzzy black wrap, I like to think of the sweet, sleeping faces of two kids and their pregnant mom. That's the kind of caring that makes getting older worthwhile. Such moments of boomerang joy make me glad I'm aging—and hoping to do it with grace.

UPLIFTER

You will be like a well-watered garden, like a spring whose waters never fail.

ISAIAH 58:11

WAY TO PRAY

Father in heaven, thank You for the years You've given me. Thank You for the opportunities to love and be loved. With Your help I'll keep on using them, drawing from that reservoir of strengthening laughter and kindness. Amen.

ANTICIPATE THE BEST!

*We spend our lives dreaming of the future,
not realizing that a little of it slips away every day.*

When my publisher called one winter morning to tell me that sales of my book *Stick a Geranium in Your Hat* had reached one million units, the head of the sales department invited Bill and me to fly to the company headquarters, all expenses paid, for a big blowout celebration. "Oh, that won't be necessary," Bill, my homebody husband, assured the executive. "Barb and I can just celebrate at home."

That afternoon he left the house whistling a merry tune and wearing an assured expression on his face. He was a man with a mission, setting off to create a celebration suitable for marking this unexpected accomplishment. While he was gone, my mind was filled with fantasy, wondering what he would bring home as his surprise for me. I pictured something sparkly, maybe a ring with a gem, or a little diamond bracelet. When he'd been gone more than two hours, I imagined him speaking to the maître d' of some fancy restaurant, setting up a lavish meal to celebrate this special occasion.

Just as I was about to burst with excited anticipation, Bill walked in the door, still whistling but now wearing a look of smug satisfaction. "Here you are," he said proudly, handing me a plastic grocery bag. "Two bundles of fresh asparagus. I know how you love it."

I looked in the bag. Sure enough. There were two perfect green bundles of my favorite vegetable. Bill had spent two hours driving from store to store, trying to find this out-of-season delicacy. "It's pretty expensive this time of year," he said, beaming, "but I figured you deserved it."

"Thanks, Mr. Wumphee," I said, more than a little surprised to be receiving asparagus instead of *carats* but genuinely touched by his thoughtfulness. "That was really nice of you."

Sometimes anticipation builds up our expectations to nearly bursting—and then reality sets in and our expectations fade out like the sorrowful sound of steam escaping from a cooling kettle. That's what happened when our four boys were young and we all piled into the family car one summer to drive from our home in southern California to visit relatives in Minnesota. On the edge of the desert, about eighty miles from home, we passed an unusual motel that caught the boys' attention. The "rooms" were shaped and painted like colorful wigwams or teepees, and the boys thought it would be the greatest thing in the world to get to spend the night there and sleep in one of those wigwams.

They were so excited about it that I promised them we would spend the night there on our way back home, even though it was less than a hundred miles from our house. They eagerly predicted how much fun it would be to sleep in such an unusual place, how it must look inside, where each

Boomerang Toy

of them would sleep, and what it would be like to tell their friends they had slept in a wigwam. Throughout the trip they reminded me of my promise. There was no way I was going to drive by that place on the way back without stopping!

Finally we headed home, and by the time the wigwam hotel came into sight, the boys were beside themselves with anticipation. "We're there!" one of them shouted as soon as the long poles poking out of the roofs appeared on the horizon.

I checked us in, and the boys scrambled out of the station wagon and soon were fighting over who got to hold the key and unlock the wigwam door. But as soon as the door swung open, the boys' faces fell.

The room was cramped and dark. The carpeting was threadbare in some spots, crusty in others. The window-unit air conditioner that protruded from the wall had long ago given up on cooling the 110-degree desert air, and there was no TV or even a bathroom—just a sink in one corner of the room. We would have to traipse one hundred feet away to a community bathroom.

It was one of the longest nights our family ever endured, with all our hot, sweaty, unbathed bodies crowded into that hot, windowless room. We were so eager to get out of that awful place that we were all awake before dawn, and for once the boys were actually waiting in the car before I even had the suitcases loaded.

When I think of the way eager anticipation has ended in disappointing reality so many times in my life, I'm thankful to remember that there's one place I can anticipate going to that will be even *better* than I expect. I can't even imagine all the wonderful things that are waiting for me there. And I know my home is there, prepared for me, grander than anything on earth, because God Himself has told me so. With all my heart I long to be there, safe in God's heaven, singing praises with His angels, thrilled beyond earthly imagination to be in His eternal presence.

I hope to see you there!

UPLIFTER

No eye has seen, no ear has heard, no mind has conceived what God has prepared for those who love him.

1 CORINTHIANS 2:9

WAY TO PRAY

Dear heavenly Father, help me see the bigger picture. When people and things disappoint, I know there is a grand plan with a higher purpose than my pleasure. If I wait, I will know joy that never quits. Help me lean into Your will and be filled with Your presence in the meantime. Amen.

THOSE STRUGGLE MUSCLES

If I had my life to live again,
I'd make the same mistakes, only sooner.

Children need to experience small failures and setbacks so they can learn how to pick themselves up and try again. We all have struggle muscles to develop. If you constantly take care of problems for your kids, you will train them in weakness, allowing their character to atrophy.

The great president Theodore Roosevelt, described as "a steam engine on two legs," was asthmatic as a little boy, not expected to live beyond age four. In the middle of dark nights, when Teddy would gasp desperately for breath, his father would pick him up and carry him outside—walking around for hours or riding in the horse carriage. In the arms of his father the small boy felt safe. The choking subsided as he gulped in fresh air and rested against a strong shoulder. His father was always there, protecting and nurturing him.

But the day came when Theodore Sr. took Teddy aside and told him, "Beating this thing is up to you now, Son. Your mind is strong but you need to develop your body." His father helped Teddy live an active life involving strenuous exercise, outdoor activities, hunting, and sport of all kinds.

Teddy threw himself into everything with determination and abandon. As he grew taller, his chest expanded and his neck thickened. He disciplined his mind and body. He was developing struggle muscles on his own. Years later those muscles helped him survive life's tragedies. Brokenhearted as a young adult by the death of the father he adored, the dark night came when both his beautiful wife and his mother died within hours of each other. Teddy left Boston and headed for the badlands of North Dakota, where he took on the rugged life of a mountain cowboy. Although a refined Easterner, Teddy gained the respect and admiration of the toughest men riding the range. Today his granddaughter says, "If it were not for that badlands experience, he would never have had what it takes to be president."

Our lives seem ordinary compared with Teddy Roosevelt's. But are we really so different? Think of the way our heavenly Father carries us through the hard times, providing comfort in those gasping, choking moments, helping us to breathe again. As we survive and grow, He challenges us to take up the fight ourselves, providing the tools to flex and grow strong. Do we do our part, trusting His Word, continuing to practice the spiritual disciplines? Do we work to the maximum of our ability? Are we determined to fight the good fight of faith?

Some say Teddy never got over the death of his wife and his mother. And yet, developing his struggle muscles in the badlands, he went on to remarry, father six children, and lead a great country through some of the worst years of its history.

We can be paralyzed by our setbacks, angry and bitter, or challenged by them to make the world a better place. The trouble with people today is that we have too many cabooses and not enough engines. Teddy was an engine. He wanted to stand in his father's shoes, so he used the tools his father provided to defeat adversity. He made sure the shoes fit.

Several years ago Oprah Winfrey got rid of an entire wardrobe; one woman bought a pair of her four-hundred-dollar shoes for five dollars. Later that same woman told Oprah she was having a difficult time raising her children on her own, but then she added, "Sometimes when I feel I can't make it, I go in the closet and I stand in your shoes."

We may feel small and spiritually asthmatic, but God is there, allowing us to grow our struggle muscles. He knows we'll need them to live out the glorious destiny He has planned for us. He has already dreamed up a great dream and a brilliant future for us. But to fulfill our potential, we need to be strong enough to fight, overcome, and love others into His kingdom.

So go for it! Lift those spiritual weights. Box with the phantoms that haunt your soul. Run hard. Get used to rough riding in Satan's badlands. Don't be afraid of mistakes or defeats; they are building blocks for all your successes. Remember, determination and faithfulness are the nails used to build the house of God's dreams.

UPLIFTER

For I know the thoughts that I think toward you, says the LORD, thoughts of peace and not of evil, to give you a future and a hope.

JEREMIAH 29:11 NKJV

WAY TO PRAY

Dear Lord, sometimes I feel so weak, but I refuse to give up. Please help me know Your presence. You are running alongside me. You love me enough to allow me to struggle for muscle. Then I will be strong and You will lead me into Your great dream. Amen.

HUMBLE JOY

My karma just ran over my dogma.

In this crazy world it's nice to know that some people still perform commonplace work with dignity, holding the world together with old-fashioned, down-home virtues. Examples are all around us. Folks still hold tight to faith in hard times. And when life pours success upon them, they just continue on, humble and kind.

It had been a long night of painting for Precious Moments artist Sam Butcher. As daylight brought busloads of tour groups to the Chapel in Carthage, Missouri, many people recognized the artist at work and began asking for his autograph. After several hours of signing, Sam finally climbed into his car and headed home through the rain.

Just outside the Precious Moments property he spotted a van on the road. Several women were standing beside it, staring dejectedly at a flat tire. Sam pulled in behind and got out to assess the situation. They needed a different jack, so he got one from his trunk and sat down in the mud to change the tire. The driver explained she had brought her church group all the way from Pennsylvania to see the Precious Moments Chapel "down the road."

"Have you ever been there?" she asked.

Sam nodded.

The lady said, "This has been a perfect trip except for one thing. Just as we were ready to leave, we learned the artist was signing figurines. We wanted so badly to have some things signed, but the lines were long and we couldn't get near him. We just had to get back home. Now here we are with a flat tire!"

"That's too bad," Sam said, finishing his work. "As soon as I wipe my hands, I'll be happy to sign anything you have."

The lady's mouth dropped open. "You?" she exclaimed. "You're the artist Sam Butcher? Why would an important person like you stop to change a tire?"

Sam replied, "Because it's flat!"

Obligingly he signed each item they handed him, leaving the ladies smiling in the rain. That flat tire had boomeranged on a group of women from Pennsylvania—and brought them joy.

Anytime we stop to care for others in their trouble, we carry the opportunity to bring boomerang joy, as surely as Sam Butcher carried the car jack those ladies needed. You don't have to be famous or important. You don't have to be acclaimed or much sought after. Just be you. Stay true to yourself and those values that keep you grounded in kindness.

Keep looking for the boomerang surprise in your life. Listen for the whirring sound that means it may be getting close. Always stay connected to people and seek out things that bring you joy. Dream with abandon. Pray confidently. But be careful what you pray for—because everything and anything is possible through the power of prayer!

UPLIFTER

Give, and it will be given to you. A good measure, pressed down, shaken together and running over, will be poured into your lap. For with the measure you use, it will be measured to you.

LUKE 6:38

WAY TO PRAY

Dear Father, I love the way You surprise me with joy. Life is never a tedious treadmill to the one who knows You. Keep me loving people and doing good. I intend to give a full measure to the world as long as I live in it. And I need Your joy! Amen.

GOD'S TEAR BOTTLE

Before you can dry another's tears, you too must weep.

Not long ago I went to the doctor, complaining that my eyes hurt. It seems I travel so much that the atmosphere on airplanes tends to dry my tear ducts. The doctor recommended artificial tears to moisturize my eyes. I laughed, amazed that I would have to buy artificial tears in a bottle, when for years I couldn't stop them from flowing! Those were the days when I took great comfort in the Scripture that assures us God collects our tears in *His* bottle (Ps. 56:8 KJV).

Frederick Buechner said, "Whenever you find tears in your eyes, especially unexpected tears, it is well to pay close attention." Why then do we so often battle our tears and struggle to keep them at bay? One woman describes tearful episodes as a freight train arriving at the wrong time and place or as outlaws shouting, "It's a holdup!" She feels ambushed by her tears.

Even on happy occasions tears can take us by surprise or make us feel ashamed. Many of us cry at happy endings, at weddings and graduations, or at the successful outcomes of traumatic events. But some scientists claim there is no such thing as tears of happiness. They claim we cry not because we are feeling positive emotions but just the opposite. They explain it takes enormous energy to repress our tears. Then, seeing the happiness of others, pent-up sadness and anxiety are discharged. In life, happy endings are the exception, and when one occurs, it stirs up anxieties about the past, they say. The experts claim that each of us is selfish and demanding, that when we cry at weddings, we are really crying for our own contrasting unhappiness. We cry because the real world isn't as happy as the one we want to see.

I'm not sure I agree, because I believe the world is shaped by the hand of a loving God. The Bible shows that we are an Easter people living in a Good Friday world, not Good Friday people living in an Easter world. That means we are destined for joy no matter how difficult our daily life. Something in us responds to the happiness others experience, because we glimpse life as God intends it to be! It is an image imprinted in the spirit of Easter morning—pure, powerful, and potent, like the Resurrection.

So go out there and help create all the happy endings you can. Don't be afraid of tears—your own or those of neighbors, family, friends, or strangers. You will have your share of Good Fridays, but Easter will come. Remember, moist eyes are good. Trembling lips are acceptable. Quivering voices won't hurt anybody. Though tears may disorient some people or send others running for cover, they communicate without words. They are signals that there is something deeper to be understood.

If you are crying, it is a sign that your heart is still tender. If your heart has been broken, you can be thankful that it is still beating and that your feelings have not been shut off.

When a song or a book moves you to tears, be glad that the writer has expanded your emotional universe. If you are shedding tears of anger or even hatred, the tears are lubricating, softening your rage. Don't let anyone or anything rip off your tender heart. It is one of the most precious resources you have. Go ahead, feel deeply and let the tears flow. But know too that the blue of heaven is far bigger than gray clouds beneath.

Let your life be rich in tears: tears of compassion when you see a malnourished child suffering on TV; tears of sadness when someone you love is ill; tears of fear and hurt, physical or emotional; tears when you are disappointed, in despair, disillusioned. Let tears of regret, renewal, and rejoicing flow. And don't forget that the most efficient water power in the world is a child's tears. Even crocodile tears! (Where did that expression come from, anyway?)

What kinds of things move you to tears? Are you crying right now? Remember, your tears are precious to God. They are like stained-glass windows in the darkness, whose true beauty is revealed only when there is a light within.

UPLIFTER

Jesus wept.

JOHN 11:35

WAY TO PRAY

Father, sometimes I am so close to tears and afraid to let them out. Sometimes they flow and flow and I wish I could stop, but I cannot. From now on I will let them be a sign to me that You are very near. Amen.

GOTCHA!

*Keep your chin up, and you'll bang
your head on the door frame.*

W hy don't we hear more about humor in the Bible? Have you ever seen those pictures of Jesus with His head thrown back, smiling so broadly that you can almost hear His laughter? I think those who know the Bible best probably have the most developed sense of humor. Like Billy Graham's wife, Ruth, who grew up in the mission field. Before they were married, she once disguised herself as a frumpy old lady to flirt with him on their college campus. Was Billy ever surprised when she pulled off her disguise and cried, "Gotcha!"

I loved reading Erma Bombeck. She was right up my alley, laughing over things I could relate to, like this: "One exercise program has you doing entire routines while cleaning house. It sounded so simple to bend over my vacuum cleaner and extend my right leg straight behind me while I touched my head to my knee. That was just before the vacuum sucked up my nightgown, causing me to nearly pass out!"

Life never fails to getcha. The best advice in order to face each day is this: hope for the best, get ready for the worst, and then take whatever God sends. What happens when life is going great and then—whammo!—some big problem hits you, knocking you into a deep valley? You can cheer yourself with the thought that the richest soil is there because that's where the fertilizer is. Try to find the funny even in the midst of a fiasco. Keep alive the enduring hope that somewhere ahead is a blessing waiting just for you. Picture Jesus throwing His head back in laughter as He anticipates what He has in store for you. The apostle Paul said to think on things that are true, noble, just, pure, lovely, of good report. He wrote, "If there is any virtue and if there is anything praiseworthy—meditate on these things ... and the God of peace will be with you" (Phil. 4:8–9 NKJV).

Develop a windshield wiper in your mind to slosh off the bad thoughts that splash across your life. Keep driving, and you will move right out from under the cloud that shadows your life.

Yes, life can getcha—when you least expect it. But think of Mary Magdalene's face when she realized that the man who spoke her name in the garden was actually Jesus. She had seen Him die, watched His blood run down the cross, brought spices to His grave. Suddenly there He was, talking to her! A huge smile must have spread like sunlight across His face. Surely that moment was the greatest gotcha in history.

If you've watched something or someone you love pass away, take my word for it, *you will laugh again*. Hold on to your hope. Be open and anticipate a good future. The worst grave of all is that of a closed heart. And remember that turning toward laughter is always a right turn, for the sound of laughter is a sign of God's hand upon a troubled world!

UPLIFTER

But he knows the way that I take; when he has tested me, I will come forth as gold.

JOB 23:10

WAY TO PRAY

Dear God, I see You smiling today. And in spite of the trials and troubles in my life right now, I see You laughing. Knowing that You see what I do not, I don't ask for success, just the simple strength to appreciate Your timing and Your testing. I know You love me madly, gladly. Amen.

PRAYER AS OINTMENT

A lot of kneeling keeps one in good standing.

Prayer is the place where burdens are shifted. Have you ever experienced the joy of coming alongside Jesus, lining up your shoulder next to His? He puts an arm around you, pulling you close. He speaks words of life into your ears, supporting your back under the stuff you are carrying. By the end of the trail you realize the stuff has shifted. It doesn't seem so heavy anymore. Surprised, you look up to see that Jesus has gone on ahead of you, with the heaviest part of your burden squarely atop His shoulders.

For the most part, life is anything but easy. It's like an ice cream cone—just when you think you've got it licked, it drips all over you. One expert in successful living advises you to simply put your head under a pillow and scream whenever the going gets tough. But I prefer these words of advice: "Blessed are the flexible, for they shall not be bent out of shape!" Prayer is the ointment that keeps our spirits flexible and malleable in the hands of God. Use this ointment before bedtime, and you won't have to muffle that scream.

A little boy captured this truth in an essay on God.

God's second most important job is listening to prayers. An awful lot of this goes on, as some people, like preachers, pray other times besides bedtime. . . . God sees everything and hears everything and is everywhere. Which keeps Him pretty busy. So you shouldn't go wasting His time by going over your parents' heads and asking for something they said you couldn't have.

Jesus helps out by listening to prayers and seeing which things are important for God to take care of and which ones He can take care of Himself without having to bother God. You can pray anytime you want and They are sure to hear you, because They've got it worked out so one of Them is on duty all the time.

God is always on duty in the temple of your heart, His home. You needn't be stiff and formal when you pray. Simply make yourself cozy in the old rocking chair of trust, pulling the afghan of faith around you, and then talk to God. It is the place where Someone takes your trouble and changes it into His treasure.

Sometimes you will find new hope bubbling to the surface. It's like watching the sunrise after a long night. But even if it's still dark when you finish praying, God is with you, reminding you that He cares. Stay in prayer. He will throw another piece of wood on the fire and pull you closer. Resist the urge to complain, because, as someone has said, the more you complain, the longer God lets you live. So pack up your gloomees in a great big box, then sit on the lid and *praise* the Lord who loves you.

God is offering Himself to you daily at a generous exchange rate: His forgiveness for your sins, His joy for your grief, His love for your loneliness. You will grow rich as you spend time with Him, listening for His voice.

"You wonder whether I understand your trouble?" He asks. "Just watch. You can't turn back the clock, but I can certainly wind it up again!"

"You ask for showers of blessing?" He asks. "Just watch, and don't forget to carry your umbrella!"

Prayer is reaching out to touch Someone—namely, your Creator. In the process He touches you. But prayer isn't magic. Jesus Himself did not come to make our suffering disappear in an instant. Instead He came to fill it with His presence. Christians are a lot like pianos—they might be square, grand, or upright, but they are no good to anyone unless they are in tune. To stay in tune with Jesus, follow His call to pray (Matt. 6:6). He promises that our Father, who sees in secret, will repay us as we do. Perhaps the Father will also *replay* us, bringing out harmonies, orchestrating magnificent chords from our suffering, making our lives a new song.

Tell God your needs and remember to thank Him for His answers. Prayer is a long-term investment, one that will increase your sense of security because God is your protector. Keep at it every day, for prayer is the key of the day and the bolt of the evening. God is waiting to hear from you.

Boomerang Joy

UPLIFTER

WAY TO PRAY

Heavenly Father, thank You for the gift of prayer. Forgive me when I don't keep in touch, allowing You to tune my life. Right now I lay myself, my duties, my burdens, small and large, at Your feet. In exchange I receive Your love and faith. Make me a fine-tuned instrument of Your peace. Amen.

HEIR-CONDITIONING

Children aren't happy with nothing to ignore,

And that's what parents were created for.

Motherhood: if it were going to be easy, it never would have started with something called *labor*. Kids can certainly test your patience—and your sense of order, too. In a last-ditch effort to save her home from total chaos, one mother resorted to putting little reminder notes all over her house.

> Inside the refrigerator: "There is no known sea green food. If noticed, please remove it before it walks away."
>
> In the bedrooms: "Having to make your beds is not considered child abuse."
>
> On the dryer: "Match every sock with something; color or pattern not important."
>
> In the family room: "Items of clothing do not have wheels. They must be carried (to your closets)."
>
> In the bathroom: "Flushing is an equal opportunity job; please press firmly on lever."
>
> On the tub: "Brand-new studies reveal that soap, when submerged in water, will dissolve!"

Parenting is relentless. We keep waiting for it to get easier, but it doesn't. If you are a parent afflicted with hardening of the attitudes, certain you're *always* right, you will identify with the mother who searched a Hallmark store for the "I told you so!" card section. If you've assumed the role of Grand Potentate over the years, it's time to abdicate. Ask yourself, *Will my being right actually change the course of history?* Take a giant leap and admit the obvious: it's wrong to always be right. Children do not care how much you know until they know how much you care.

When things are bad between you and your children, take comfort in the thought that things could be even worse. Believe me, I know! And when they *are* worse, find hope in the fact that things can only get better. This parenting business is tough. For stress relief now, take a little nap or a long walk. And keep your sense of humor handy—like a needle and thread, it will patch up so many things!

Kids are always learning, from everything you *aren't* trying to teach. They learn, for example, that after a kid stops believing in Santa Claus, a kid gets underwear for Christmas. Resist the temptation to argue. Listen to your kids and learn what's really on their minds.

Remember that patience is the ability to idle your motor when you feel like stripping your gears. Being a parent also means working without a net. Even if you're scared to death, you have to keep going, looking straight ahead and always looking up. Try to brighten *up* a room, polish *up* the silver, and lock *up* the house while your kids work *up* appetites, think *up* excuses, and stir *up* trouble. Before you had them, you believed the old saying that children brighten up a home. Now you know they do, because they never turn off the lights! There is nothing more secure for either parent or child than knowing and loving the heavenly Father above. Now that's a real picker-upper!

When you decided to become a mother, you gave your heart permission to forever walk around outside your body. When that little wiggling child was placed in your arms, you knew nothing would ever be the same again. As kids change and grow, come and go, just keep the hearth fires burning. And remember that mothers should be like quilts, keeping kids warm without smothering them.

For their part, kids are like sponges—they absorb all your strength and leave you limp, but give them a squeeze and you get it all back! And let's face it: child rearing is a pretty cool job—the biggest "heir-conditioning" job ever!

UPLIFTER

Do not forget the things your eyes have seen or let them slip from your heart as long as you live. Teach them to your children and to their children after them.

DEUTERONOMY 4:9

WAY TO PRAY

God, You've given me these beautiful gifts, my kids! They are so maddeningly sweet and confusing, lovable and irritating, smart and foolish, all at the same time! Show me how to raise them in You, to always find a way back to You. Thank You for the joy and the trials, too. I love them (and You). Amen.

TRY THE UPLOOK

*An optimist is a gal who can always see
the bright side of other people's problems.*

God put me on earth to accomplish a certain number of things. But right now I am so far behind, I figure I will never die. Bill and I live in a mobile home park, where we have our ministry office, in which we host thousands of "visitors" yearly. Most of these arrive in the guise of handwritten letters from people who have read my books. Boy, do they keep me busy! A typical letter may detail family difficulties and then say something like this: "I start getting these sinking feelings and wonder how I will ever get through it." Well, families are like fudge—mostly sweet with a few nuts. We all have bumpy people in our lives. Sometimes because of that, *insanity* is our only means of relaxation—isn't it?

Today I read through a few of the letters—again. What strikes me is how varied the troubles are and how deep the pain. But then I remember that pain can be the sign of a sensitive heart. You can only be hurt if you care a lot. As Mother Teresa put it, "A living love hurts." Caring is a gift you give the other person. And Christian women are good at caring. The pain that sometimes results is a value-added premium to let you know that you are alive and well, that you still have a tender heart.

As I write this today, my finger is bleeding all over the typewriter keys. Last weekend I helped a single mom move. Sweeping her floor, I found something too big for the vacuum cleaner and picked it up. I didn't realize I had just tucked a tiny razor into my pocket! Today I put on the slacks I wore that day, then stuck my hands in my pockets. Fresh out of bandages, I've wrapped my now throbbing finger with tissue and scotch tape. But the cut is deeper than I thought. I begin to work (deadlines call!) even though my finger is still bleeding.

The letters I read as I write are now streaked with real blood, a symbol of tender broken hearts. The letter writers have no idea they are not as alone as they think. They don't realize they are part of a sisterhood of women who hurt and bleed, all because they care enough to love. My small hurt helps me identify with their pain, and I remember that sympathy is nothing other than *your* pain in *my* heart.

We cannot always head off disaster. Sometimes we discover that the light at the end of the tunnel really is the headlight of an oncoming train. Even so, Satan will not get the victory. Christian women will keep on risking their hearts whatever happens.

My makeshift bandages don't last long. But at last the bleeding tapers off. My finger is healing itself. In the same way, God mends broken hearts, with time and care.

Bill and I tell people, "When the outlook is poor, try the uplook; God has His hand on you." Many of these letter writers order books and tapes, asking us to send them in plain brown envelopes. As parents of gay children, they often feel so alone and ashamed. We tell them, "Openness is to whole-ness as secrets are to sickness." And we stay in touch with them through a monthly newsletter, which I write, Bill prints, and we both staple, fold, stuff, seal, and zip code. When we take it to the post office, we pray for each one as we mail it, that it will be a lifeline to people in pain.

Bill and I receive no salary or bonus, but the perks we get are fabulous! We get the satisfaction of letters assuring us that our ministry of encouragement is really working. And we get all kinds of fun stuff for our crazy joy room, too. In giving it *away,* joy has boomeranged!

I've found that the best thing to hold on to in this life is each other. When even that fails, we can be assured that God is holding on to us. I try to take the cold water thrown upon me, heat it with enthusiasm, and use the steam to push ahead. On the long journey, I seek to love and to live in the strength of the Lord.

Some days I actually do get my act together, but then the curtain comes down! Reality is so daily. So I often tell God, "I don't mind the rat race, but I could do with a little more cheese, please."

At the end of each day, before turning down the covers, I turn all my problems over to the Holy Spirit—every last one. I'm grateful He stays up late to handle them. Then I lay down, secure in the knowledge that broken things become blessed things if I let Christ do the mending!

UPLIFTER

With joy you will draw water from the wells of salvation. In that day you will say: "... Shout aloud and sing for joy."

ISAIAH 12:3–4, 6

WAY TO PRAY

Dear heavenly Father, You've given me so many opportunities to find joy in hidden places. I look for seeds of joy as on a treasure hunt. Please bless me and bless my sisters in faith whose bleeding still won't stop despite the bandages. Thank You that pain is a sign we are still alive, still loving. No one can rob us of that. Amen.

SEASON OF JOY

Each day comes bearing its gifts.
Out part is to untie the ribbons.

Christmas shopping! When do you start this annual chore? I know women who begin the day after Christmas. They buy up decorations and other holiday supplies for better than half price and scour picked-over racks and shelves for gifts. They make crafts all through the winter, hiding them away for the next year. Their Christmas preparations are complete by the beginning of summer! And they enjoy December with their families beside a cozy fireplace.

Other people finally make it to the largest mall in town by mid-December. They wouldn't miss the hurly-burly mood of holiday shopping, including bell-ringing Santas and brightly decorated windows. Then there are those who don't manage to get their cards mailed before Ground Hog Day! If by a miracle they do get it done before Christmas Eve, they triumphantly announce, "This is the earliest I've ever been late!"

Wouldn't you love to simplify the season by finding one gift perfect for everybody on your list? Something personal and practical that doesn't need dusting, can be used immediately, fits perfectly, and lasts forever and a day? One lady said she found it: gift certificates for a flu shot! Another lady gave her weight-watching friends a hand-lettered list of advantages to being chubby during the holidays.

1. You don't need padding for your Santa suit.
2. You don't need as much water to fill your bath.
3. You don't have to buy your clothes in the rap music department.
4. And there's so much more of you to love!

How they all must have appreciated that!

For many people the holidays are not so jolly. Everybody knows Christmas is supposed to be the season of joy. But it doesn't always feel like it. Do visions of holiday celebrations fill your heart with warm anticipation—or dread? Even for the best of families, all may not be calm and bright. The pressure of expectations, our own and others', often sets us up for disappointment and stress that can sabotage our joy. We remember our losses most keenly during such times of traditional celebration.

Holidays are full of contradictions, and it's OK if our celebrations are, too. Our rituals and traditions express good feelings and sad feelings, but they still enhance our family life. Being real about what we feel helps everybody heal. Since women are the holiday ritual makers, it's good to keep this in mind. Your Christmas doesn't have to look like something out of *Victoria* magazine or a Norman Rockwell painting.

Perhaps it will be closer to a painting by Thomas Kinkade. In his paintings light streams from the windows of cozy cottages or churches onto the world outside. He never lets us peek inside, so we don't know what's happening behind closed doors. We only know that the people who live there are living in the light. And we see that light spreading beyond their walls, like an invitation to warmth and fun.

Picture-perfect images? Nothing has to be the way you grew up thinking it should be! Don't feel that this Christmas you have to do everything you've always done, the way you've always done it. Each year create one or two new traditions; try to find ideas that suit your family better than things you did the year before. Encourage the voices, opinions, and wishes of your children, no matter how young. Go for family feeling but keep it simple. What makes your children laugh? Warms the heart of your spouse? Tickles your fancy? The best things are not expensive. The best things come from the heart.

As Christians, we know the reason for the season. Bethlehem's stable was the first step in God's love journey to Calvary's cross. Jesus came in winter, when the world was at its darkest, to a people living under the heel of a cruel Roman empire. Welcoming that Christmas baby into such a place and time must have taken faith on Mary and Joseph's part. Jesus came bringing His own joy when the world had none to spare. He came shining His own light.

There is always a light in the darkness. Look for it; believe in it. The love of God is shining through the darkest night, brighter than a Kinkade painting. Then get ready for Christmas. Look into the Father's face, tell Him you receive His gift, and then untie the ribbons!

UPLIFTER

In him was life, and that life was the light of men.

JOHN 1:4

WAY TO PRAY

Dear Lord, Your love is like a fire. It brings warmth, light, and peace to my dark places. Your fire both energizes and settles my spirit. By its glow I snuggle closer to You. Thank You for Your Christmas gift. One day we will celebrate forever, and there will be no tears, only forever joy! Amen. Come soon, Lord Jesus!

HUG-A-DAY CLUB

> *Hugging is a miracle drug; look for an*
> *overworked, overdrawn, overlooked, overwrought*
> *(but basically fun) person and give 'em a squeeze!*

A hug can relieve tension, improve blood flow, reduce stress, boost self-esteem, and generate goodwill. Hugs cure a lot more than whatever ails you. They keep you immune to illness of the mind. A hug is a tranquilizer with no side effects. What else? A hug requires no batteries, is nontaxable, nonpolluting, extremely personal, fully returnable, and available at absolutely no cost! (P.S.: It is recommended for ages one to one hundred—and up.)

Give hugs away, and you're likely to get one back. But like it or not, sometimes you have to give yourself a hug! One lady I read about was planning a romantic evening the day her husband returned from a hunting trip. As he was unpacking his bag in the bedroom, she heard him say, "Oh, baby, did I miss you!" Turning around to embrace him, she saw he was kissing the remote control! I saw a cartoon recently in which the wife was saying there are times when she can't hold her husband long enough—because she knew if she let go, he would go straight for the remote! Fortunately, self-hugs are not hard to practice. Just wrap those beautiful arms around yourself, give your back a little pat, and squeeze tight. Believe me, it works wonders!

Hugs go together with heartprints. Whatever you do that is compassionate, kind, comforting, or affectionate is a heartprint. Even if it isn't Valentine's Day, a smackaroo on the cheek might do a loved one good. An arm around someone's shoulder. A firm handshake. A kiss on the tips of the toes. A hand to hold. A full body squeeze. A tear dried with your fingertips. A playful tickle.

How many ways can you bring the touch of God's love to another person? God created us to need the touch of others. Scientists claim that normal people can feel on their fingertips or cheeks something that weighs as little as a bee's wing falling from less than half an inch away! If that is true, we are sensitive to the gentlest gestures. Each stroke registers in our brains, connecting us to a positive experience in the world. But imagine feeling only rude or harsh touches: bumps, jabs, slaps, pinches, pokes, or scrapes. That kind of touch makes you feel irritable, unsafe, even angry. And what of those who are rarely touched at all? They end up feeling invisible and are invalidated. One woman said, "I've gone to look for myself. If I should return before I get back, keep me here!" Now that is loneliness. She needs a great big hug.

The best exercise for a good relationship is to bend toward somebody else, extend your arms, and pull him or her close to you. God has "everlasting arms." When He said, "It is not good for man to be alone," I think He was thinking of hugs. Every kid should learn that life is full of hugs! It is easy to wrap a hug around a little one, because they are small and squishy. But be sure to squeeze softly. There is nobody who doesn't need a hug—even teenagers need 'em regularly, although they might need to be reminded to hug you back! You might say, "I think I need a hug ... and also a maid, a cook, a chauffeur ... and a lot more hugs!"

Some say the best way to forget your troubles is to wear tight shoes, but I say go out and hug somebody. A day without a hug is too heavy a load for anyone to carry. Sometimes a grouch needs a hug the most! It may be the sunshine that finally drives winter from his or her face.

If you get a hug, enjoy it. And when you leave for the day, always take your hug with you!

UPLIFTER

His left arm is under my head, and his right arm embraces me.
SONG OF SONGS 2:6

WAY TO PRAY

Heavenly Father, thank You for the hugs You give me through the love of family and friends. When I feel alone, remind me that the only equipment I need is my own two arms to hug someone who is even lonelier than I am. Amen.

WE'LL FLY AWAY

"Good morning! This is God. I will be handling all your problems today. I will not need your help. So have a good day!"

Several years ago my friend Dr. Walter Martin, a renowned Bible teacher, was invited to appear on the Phil Donahue program to talk about death and the afterlife. The other guest was an expert on reincarnation and spiritism. The discussion about who can get to heaven progressed, but Dr. Martin was given little opportunity to talk about his views—until the end of the program. In the closing minutes Donahue came over, slipped his arm around Dr. Martin's shoulder, and patronizingly said, "Oh, Walter, come on now, don't you think that when I get to the pearly gates, God will just lean over and say, 'Oh, Phil, you're OK. Come on in'?"

Dr. Martin's face just lit up. With a big smile he replied, "Oh, but Phil, He already did! He invited you into His kingdom more than nineteen hundred years ago, paid your penalty, and offered you eternal life! The choice is up to you!" Phil Donahue was taken back by Dr. Martin's answer. I still get choked up when I remember that moment. It was the high point of the show.

Earthly life is but seventy years, or eighty if we have the strength, says Psalm 90:10. "They quickly pass, and we fly away." Isn't that a fantastic hope? I sometimes wonder why people like Phil Donahue don't grasp it. We will fly away! I love an old song that encourages us to "lift up our heads ... our redemption draws nigh." We are pilgrims on earth, not settlers. We can't take anything with us, but we can surely send it on ahead!

I'll never forget the plaque that hung on the dining room wall of my childhood home:

Only one life, twill soon be past
Only what's done for Christ will last.

How true that is. Our time here is preparation for our palace there. I like the bumper sticker that says, "Life is hard and then you die!" Or as my granddaughter says, "We should say life is hard and then we get to be with Jesus!" Isn't that fabulous? What's so great about this life, anyway, that you'd want to hold on to it forever? As Christians, we have an endless hope, not a hopeless end. The acrostic for HOPE is:

He
Offers
Peace
Eternal

Recently someone closed a letter addressed to me with this phrase: "Until He comes or I go!" I just loved that. Another letter closed, "Awaiting His shout!" Isn't that terrific? It makes me want to run right out and do Rapture practice. Revelation 1:7 says, "He is coming with the clouds, and every eye will see him." We should all go into the backyard and jump up and down every day, practicing for Jesus' return. When I spoke of this at a meeting, one little old lady came up to me afterward and asked, "Mrs. Johnson, when you do your Rapture practice, do you do it on a trampoline or on the grass?" It doesn't matter, I told her, because one day He is gonna toot and we are gonna scoot!

I heard about a man in Hyde Park in London who carried a sign that read, "Due to the shortage of trained trumpeters, the end of the world will be postponed three months." Well, let's not delay Jesus' coming; let's be ready! A sign on a church bulletin board said, "Interested in going to heaven? Apply here for flight training." That's the spirit!

What if you or I die before the Rapture? We know death is merely God's way of saying, "Your table is ready." Our loved ones who die are not gone; they have just gone *on ahead*. Heaven's travel agency guarantees first-class accommodations (John 14:2). We are immigrants taking up permanent residence (Heb. 11:16), admitted because our names are registered in advance (Rev. 21:27). We need declare only one thing to get through customs (1 Cor. 15:1, 3–4), but no luggage is permitted (1 Tim. 6:7). Vaccinations are not needed, as diseases are unknown at destination (Rev. 21:4). Date of departure is yet to be announced; travelers are advised to prepare to leave at short notice (Acts 1:7). Those taking direct flights are advised to watch daily for indications of imminent departure (1 Thess. 4:17).

Jesus is preparing a mansion for us there. When I am homesick for heaven, I pray, "Lord, while You're busy preparing a place for me, prepare me for that place!"

UPLIFTER

No eye has seen, no ear has heard, no mind has conceived what God has prepared for those who love him.

1 CORINTHIANS 2:9

WAY TO PRAY

PERMANENT HOOKUP

God
I am always getting one thing
Straightened out with You
And then another lion
Jumps out of the jungle.
Why couldn't You create
Some kind of permanent hookup
So life would stay
Settled, serene
And ecstatically spiritual?
Dear child
I have.
It's called Heaven.
Ruth Harms Calkin

GIVE THANKS

Frogs have it easy; they can eat whatever's bugging them.

One of my greatest joys is putting together *The Love Line,* our Spatula family newsletter—mainly because it is compiled from the letters, cards, and jokes sent to me by readers. It is a special relationship network. Donations through this newsletter have helped pay for many needs, such as transportation to bring home AIDS patients estranged from their families. This included a patient who was united with his wife and newborn baby last year. I am so thankful for the many people who have been part of this joy.

Thankfulness itself has become a boomerang theme for me, especially on bad days. Yes, I do have bad days. Like everyone else, I sometimes feel God has passed me by, put me on a shelf, or left me in a basement to languish somewhere. But even if I can't be thankful for what I've received, I've learned to be thankful for what I've escaped. One little girl was overjoyed one Thanksgiving Day because broccoli wasn't on the table! When God does make broccoli part of the menu or when he allows tears to form in my eyes, I've learned it's only because He has a greater good in mind—He wants to grow a rainbow in my heart.

I don't know about you, but I don't want to live my life in the past lane. I want to find a zillion things to be thankful for today. What are you thankful for right this moment? Gene Perret says maybe you can thank God "for bathtubs—the one place where Mom is allowed some time to herself."

Sometimes life is like a box of chocolates; other times it is a rocky road you can't even eat your way out of. Perhaps you can relate to this letter: "I have fallen and I can't get up! My worst fears have come to pass. I don't know where to go for help. I feel like such a failure. Please write and tell me what to do next." I might be tempted to say, "If all else fails, fudge it!"

Why do we take our blessings for granted until they are removed from us? Start today by being grateful for the tiniest things: water to drink, a moment to rest, the color of a flower or sunset or bird. A piece of bread. A song on the radio. Keep looking for sights, smells, sounds, that make you feel pleasure. Write them down. One woman wrote, "I've been writing at least five things I'm grateful for each night. It's been wonderful. I certainly see a change. I was such a negative person."

Let's decide to be thankful and encourage one another to cultivate grateful hearts. Remember, no trial or trouble lasts forever. Keep following God, and you will begin to understand that He uses trials to strengthen you. And also remember, the truest truth is that God is thankful for *you*. He gave his Son to reclaim your life. He invites you into the joy of salvation. That's an awful lot to be thankful for right there. And something else to be thankful for? The fact that you are here to be thankful!

UPLIFTER

I always thank God for you.

1 CORINTHIANS 1:4

WAY TO PRAY

My Lord Jesus, You have blessed me way beyond my ability to thank You. If this were a contest between Your blessing and my thankfulness, You would win hands down. Still, I'd like to try to compete by showering You with thankfulness each day. Open my eyes to all the ways You're blessing me, and I will give You thanks. Amen.

SCRAPBOOKS OF THE SOUL

↬

*I am better than I was but not
quite so good as I was before I got worse.*

Scrapbook lovers rejoice! This is your moment! Now you can put together scrapbook photo albums with stickers, stamps, and special acid-free, photo-friendly paper to commemorate life's most important moments. Your one-of-a-kind album will become a family heirloom if you take advantage of special pens, glues, photo corners, mats, page protectors, fun paper punches, and decorative-edged scissors! As for me, I love the idea of finding fresh and creative ways to treasure the moments.

Like Mary, the mother of Jesus, I have treasured many moments in my heart, special memories of God's faithfulness to my family over many years. God Himself has used all kinds of colorful and creative ways to document His love, glorify Himself, and pass on the heritage of faith through the scrapbook pages of my life. Best of all, He guarantees that none of it will fade away. It is all acid-free!

God uses something even better than stamps, stickers, and scissors. He uses that little bottle of magic stuff called White-Out!

You know, the stuff that does a fantastic job of erasing mistakes. With a dab of a brush, the wrong thing is covered over, leaving a fresh white space upon which He may write.

Years ago when I worked in an office, I called White-Out my 1 John 1:9 stuff because it would blot out the mess and leave a clean place—just like God does with our sins. We all need spiritual White-Out to make us white as snow (Isa. 1:18). We can all have a clean, fresh start every day. God no longer sees our sin, because it is covered by His special White-Out: the blood of Jesus.

In our journey through life, the scraps and souvenirs we save can be turned into artwork by the creative hand of the Lord. Let Him sit down at the table of your life and go to work. And while you're at it, why not help Him out? Gather up all the color you can. Cut away the broken ends of your life. Find "stickers of the heart"—things to make you laugh. Most of all, don't let the best you have done so far be the standard for the future. You can do even better. Let God use His White-Out; it works wonders!

UPLIFTER

If we confess our sins, he is faithful and just and will forgive us our sins and purify us from all unrighteousness.

1 JOHN 1:9

WAY TO PRAY

Almighty God, my Redeemer, thank You that the blood of Jesus cleanses me from my sin. Please send Your Holy Spirit to fill me with Your peace so I can rest in the midst of my circumstances. You have given me forgiveness and righteousness in Jesus' name. Hooray for Your heavenly White-Out! Amen.

LIVING AT GERIATRIC JUNCTION

My bifocals are adequate, my dentures fit fine.

My face-lift is holding, but I sure miss my mind!

We all know why God made it so difficult for women over fifty to have babies, don't we? Why, they would put them down someplace and forget where they left them! Of course, I only forget three things: names, faces, and ... oh dear, I forgot the third!

Men are just as bad, I guess. They forget names and faces, not to mention birthdays and anniversaries. Later on they forget to pull their zippers up, and even later they forget to pull them down! If that isn't bad enough, think of their hair problems. The reason men don't need face-lifts is because sooner or later their face will grow right up through their hair. One man I talked to said when he was young he used to wash his hair with Head and Shoulders but now he uses Mop and Glow. A friend of mine who is completely bald refuses to wear turtlenecks, certain they would make him look like a roll-on deodorant! Here's a cure for baldness you might want

"HE'S RECOVERING JUST FINE. THE ONLY
DRAWBACK HAS BEEN THAT WHEN HE
HICCUPS, THE PACEMAKER CAUSES THE
TV TO CHANGE CHANNELS."

to try: Mix one part Epsom salts to one part alum mixed with three tablespoons persimmon juice. Vigorously rub this mixture into your husband's scalp three times daily. It won't keep his hair from falling out, but it will shrink his head to fit the hair he has left!

One lady wrote about problems her husband was having as he grew older: "He's been doing dumb things," she said. "While I was away visiting my sister, he did the laundry by stuffing his dirty socks into water glasses, then putting them in the dishwasher. Then he wore the socks and drank out of the water glasses." (I warned this lady to stop visiting her sister and stick close to home.)

Another lady told me her husband just sat around with the remote in his hand. I comforted her with words I once heard someone say: "If you love something, set it free. If it returns, you haven't lost it. If it disappears, it wasn't truly yours to begin with. If it sits there watching television, unaware it's been set free, you probably already married it!"

To aging women who worry about the passing years, I say, Just relax and enjoy life, even the parts you can't remember! After all, the only way to look younger is not to be born so soon! It's impossible to fool Mother Nature, no matter how much you exercise—especially when all you exercise is *caution*.

An old-timer, of course, is anyone who learned to ride a bicycle before it became a fitness machine. My middle-aged girlfriend started an aerobics program but quit because her thighs kept rubbing together and setting her pantyhose on fire! As for me, whenever I think about exercise, I lie down until the thought goes away. My idea of strenuous exercise is to fill the bathtub and lie back, then pull the plug and fight the current. How's that for maturity?

Nowadays most of us are a lot like ducks swimming in a lake—composed on the surface but paddling like crazy underneath. Real maturity, we discover, means being gentle with the young, compassionate with the elderly, and tolerant of the weak as well as the strong—because we have been all these things at one time or another. The best way to grow in maturity is to pray this little prayer every day:

> Thank You, dear God, for all You have given me,
> for all You have taken from me, for all You have left me!

I spoke recently at a retreat for "golden-agers," folks between seventy and eighty years old. Breakfast was to be served buffet-style, with each table of ten going up for food. The table with the folks taking the most pills that morning would get to go first. That was the prize! With *seventy-two* pills (Bill and I had already taken ours in our room), our table took the honors.

As we grow older, pills and all, we need to carve out happiness and joy every day. But we can't do it by avoiding things. Trying to stave off age or trouble is like trying to nail Jell-O to a tree. We can only do it by entrusting more of ourselves to God each day.

One nice thing about the passing of years is that you and your children eventually wind up on the same side of the generation gap. You can avenge yourself on them by living long enough to cause them trouble. Another nice thing about aging is that each day you get closer to seeing the Lord. Imagine that scene! To me it has a silvery sheen; all sadness is transformed and everything dull will be made bright!

Boomerang Joy

Reynolds Wrap celebrated its fiftieth anniversary last year. The salesman who sold the first roll of aluminum foil is still alive at age eighty-four. In fifty years Reynolds produced seventy-nine million miles of the stuff, enough to stretch from the earth to the moon and back 180 times! Something about that picture reminds me of God's silvery stuff stretching from heaven to earth many times over—wrapping us in His protective love as the years pass. Because of that I'm not afraid of aging, forgetfulness, pills, or creaky bones. I just remember that growing old is mandatory but growing up is optional. I am always in my prime until I get wrinkles in my heart!

UPLIFTER

For a thousand years in your sight are like a day that has just gone by, or like a watch in the night.... Teach us to number our days aright, that we may gain a heart of wisdom.

PSALM 90:4, 12

WAY TO PRAY

Dear God, keep me unafraid of passing years. They go so quickly! I place my life in Your love. I am hid with Christ in You. Bless this body of mine and use it to bless others as long as possible. Amen.

SAIL ON, SAIL ON

*Worry is the senseless process of cluttering up
tomorrow's opportunities with leftover problems from today.*

With a seventy-pound duffel bag slung over his shoulder, a young airman en route to his first assignment headed up the gangplank and was escorted to the "stateroom." One hundred canvas cots, a small pillow and blanket on each, were stacked four high and squeezed into that hold. As the vessel sailed away from the dock and into the wide Pacific Ocean, there was a lump in the young man's throat.

The ship sailed eleven days through all kinds of weather. In smooth waters the sea was like glass. In storms the waves rocked and rolled the ship like a toy in a whirlpool. At one point the propeller actually came out of the water, vibrating the walls of the ship so hard that the crew worried it would bust apart. When the first day of seasickness hit, the airman wanted to die. The second day brought only regret that he hadn't. The third day finally brought a little hope. Like Jonah, the young airman looked back on his ordeal as the defining experience of his life, remembering God's promise to be faithful and to hold His children fast.

We are engraved on the palm of God's hand, says one of the prophets. He has made an irrevocable commitment to care for us, a promise that will last to the end of time. In our world, enduring commitments are rare. I am reminded of the hen and her friend the pig, strolling down the avenue. The hen spotted a huge billboard advertising breakfast. "Look at those beautiful eggs with the bright yellow yolks!" she said. The pig responded, "Yes, and look at that marvelous fried ham steak!" Then the pig thought for a moment and began to look troubled. "Wait a minute! For you breakfast is just a contribution; for me it's total commitment!"

But the model for total commitment is Jesus Himself. He died that we might live! And the Father kept His commitment by raising Him up. How then can we doubt that God is for us?

For anyone who has ever been abandoned, abused, or mistreated by an earthly parent, the realization of the Father's faithfulness can send shock waves of joy through the soul. But it takes a willingness to unlearn old lessons. I heard about a four-year-old boy on an outing with his father. As crowds rushed about in the huge train depot, the boy did not notice as his father let go of his hand. Suddenly the boy grabbed hold of a jacket sleeve, smiled up at his father, but saw instead the gnarled face of a stranger who pulled roughly away. Frightened, the boy looked around and then spotted his father hiding behind a post, laughing at him. From that moment he grew angry and ashamed. His father had let him down, and he would never trust him again. That boy needed to unlearn the lesson he learned that day, in order to trust the unwavering compassion and protection of his heavenly Father.

Sometimes the lines of our lives get tangled by other people, but God is there as we wriggle in pain. He says, "Be still, dear, while I untie the knot!" He never promises smooth sailing, but He does promise to be at the helm of our ship. I like the old saying that goes like this:

> All the water in the world, however hard it tried,
> Could never sink a ship unless it got inside.
> All the evil in the world, the wickedness and sin,
> Can never sink your soul's fair craft unless you let it in.

Did you know that an opal is a stone with a broken heart? Made of dust, sand, and silica, it is full of minute fissures that allow air inside. The trapped air refracts the light, resulting in the lovely hues of color that inspired the opal's nickname: the Lamp of Fire. When kept in a cold, dark place, the opal loses its luster. But when held in a warm hand or when the light shines on it, the luster is restored. So it is with us. A broken heart becomes a lamp of fire when we allow God to breathe on it and warm us with His life.

If things are tough, remember that every flower that ever bloomed had to go through a whole lot of dirt to get there. The almighty Father will use life's reverses to move you forward. So do not keep grieving about a bitter experience. The present is slipping by while you are regretting the past and worrying about the future. Regret will not prevent tomorrow's sorrows; it will only rob today of its strength. So keep on believing. With Jesus you have not a hopeless end but an endless hope!

God knows exactly how much you can take, and He will never permit you to reach a breaking point. He will not twist your arm or let go of your hand. He is stitching your sails with love. His work takes time but it will never unravel in a storm. So whether you're sailing the high seas or floundering in the pits, know that *yesterday* is just experience but *tomorrow* is glistening with purpose—and *today* is the channel leading from one to the other. Sail on boldly and bravely. For the Father in heaven will never leave the helm of your ship!

UPLIFTER

If I rise on the wings of the dawn, if I settle on the far side of the sea, even there your hand will guide me, your right hand will hold me fast.
PSALM 139:9–10

WAY TO PRAY

Father, people have failed me but You never will. I hold fast to that truth as You hold fast to me. Amen.

THE GUILT-FREE LIFE

*Being codependent means that when you die,
someone else's life passes before your eyes.*

Guilt! Don't we all deal with it? Whether it's true guilt, false guilt, or misplaced guilt, it's hard to shake. The psalmist wrote, "What happiness for those whose guilt has been forgiven!" (Ps. 32:1 LB). Why then are there so many guilt-ridden Christians who have lost their joy?

Do you feel guilty about feeling so guilty? We know that once we are born again, God cannot see our sin, because it has been covered by the blood of Jesus. Remember that and learn to accept your failures and mistakes, being honest with God about them. Come to Him on His terms. He knows you're not perfect, so go ahead and admit it to yourself.

God loves you so much that He accepts you as you are. But He loves you far too much to leave you that way! Reach out for God's forgiveness in the name of Jesus. Accept the fact that you stand pure and innocent in His presence. How many of us suffer needlessly because we are too proud to live by grace? We try and try and try, but we strive only in our own power. Some of us approach every situation as a life-and-death matter. We "die" a lot more often than we need to. But Jesus already did that for us! Don't insult the Father's love by rejecting the forgiveness He offers through His Son.

A little girl once prayed, "God, when You forgive, do You use an eraser?" The Bible says He wipes out our sin entirely. He removes it as far as the east is from the west. How far is that? It is a divine riddle; I don't know the answer. I only know that when I pray, "Lord, I have a problem; it's me," He responds, "Barbara, I have the answer; it's Me!"

Jesus admonished us to be perfect (Matt. 5:48). *What?* Did He really mean *perfect?* Somebody once said that the only way to achieve perfection is to make mistakes when no one else is present! But God is always present. Only through the saving work of Christ are we made perfect to God. He gives us grace and spiritual gifts to work out our salvation. The difference between our efforts and the efforts of nonbelievers is that we strive in the abundant grace of God.

Do you want to know what a difference a little extra effort can make? If 99.9 percent accuracy is good enough, two million documents will be lost by the IRS this year, twelve babies will be given to the wrong parents each day, and over three hundred entries in the next edition of Webster's Dictionary will turn out to be misspelled. More examples? Consider these slight errors in the wording and punctuation of announcements that have appeared in church bulletins.

- Don't let worry kill you—let the church help.
- For those of you who have children and don't know it, we have a nursery downstairs.
- At the evening service tonight, the sermon topic will be "What Is Hell?" Come early and listen to our choir practice.

Yes, errors do happen. But mistakes offer the possibility for redemption and a new start in God's kingdom. No matter what you're guilty of, God can restore your innocence. As you place yourself under the sovereign lordship of Jesus Christ, each mistake or failure can lead you right back to the throne. So strive to be perfect, but do it joyfully, because God's grace is the only power strong enough to make you so.

UPLIFTER

Blessed is he whose transgressions are forgiven, whose sins are covered. Blessed is the man whose sin the LORD does not count against him and in whose spirit is no deceit.

PSALM 32:1–2

WAY TO PRAY

Dear Lord, here I am, fully aware of my faults and short-comings. I confess my lack of faith in Your transforming grace. I want to start again. Accept my humble efforts and my love for You. Thank You for salvation in Your Son, Jesus. Amen.

JUST A LITTLE HOPE

Hope is a wonderful thing—
one little nibble will keep a man fishing all day.

When a neighbor needs help, you just give it, knowing it's the right thing to do." That's what one woman said when a twister struck her small town. Hundreds of people whose homes had been spared reached out to help less fortunate neighbors.

In another town a single mom was told she had only thirty days to buy the house she lived in; otherwise she would be evicted. Suddenly her dreams for her family were dashed. On the other side of town another woman felt an urge to call that very day just to say hello. That one call changed both their lives forever. "It was apparent she had been crying," the caller later explained, "so she told me about the eviction. I knew that what happened to them could happen to any one of us." A simple plan was hatched that day to save the family's home.

You never know who needs a bit of human kindness *right now*. A note or letter of encouragement may be all that is needed. If you feel the urge to reach out, don't procrastinate, because tomorrow may be too late.

One woman went to her doctor to get the results of a checkup. The doctor said, "I have good news and bad news. Which do you want first?"

She answered, "The good news!"

The doctor said, "You have twenty-four hours to live."

"Good grief," exclaimed the woman. "That's the *good* news? Then what's the *bad* news?"

"The bad news," replied the doctor, "is that I was supposed to tell you yesterday."

Even able-bodied, self-sufficient people treasure small gestures of kindness. Proverbs 12:25 says, "An anxious heart weighs a man down, but a kind word cheers him up." You might write a card recalling a sweet memory you once shared with someone going through a hard time. You might remind a sick friend of how their own past kindness can strengthen them now. Or you might simply list all the positive qualities of a son or daughter or spouse. If you hate to write, clip out stories and cartoons, or pop a few autumn leaves or pressed flowers into an envelope and mail them to a friend. Make a special meal for someone who is hurting. Join a bake sale— and remember that charity is when you make cookies for a worthy cause; compassion is when you buy them back.

Nowadays we are so busy, it's hard to find time to do something thoughtful. You have to slice the time from your schedule. If you do, encouragement will come boomeranging into your own backyard! One of Sweden's past queens once sold her jewels to build hospitals and orphanages throughout the country. Years later as she visited one of these places, tears from a bedridden woman fell glistening onto the queen's hand. She exclaimed, "God is sending me back my jewels!"

Paul wrote: "I urge you … to offer your bodies as living sacrifices, holy and pleasing to God" (Rom. 12:1). Now, we all know that the problem with being a living sacrifice is that it's so easy to crawl off the altar. Don't do it. Commit yourself to being a hope bringer no matter what. Hope looks for the good in people, opens doors for people, discovers what can be done to help, lights a candle, does not yield to cynicism. Hope sets people free:

A gracious word may smooth the way,
A joyous word may make one's day!

I recently read about a survey in which ninety-five-year-olds were asked, "If you could live your life over, what would you do differently?" The old people mentioned two things: "We would reflect more" and "We would do more things that would last beyond our lifetime."

Don't let your life speed out of control. Live intentionally. Do something today that will last beyond your lifetime. People can live for up to seventy days without food, ten days without water, and six minutes without air. But they can't live without hope. Be grateful today for the hope you've been given and then find creative ways to pass it on to someone else.

UPLIFTER

Because of the LORD's great love we are not consumed, for his compassions never fail. They are new every morning.

LAMENTATIONS 3:22–23

WAY TO PRAY

Our heavenly Father, thank You for being the source of everything worth living for. Give me ideas and energy to bring Your kind of hope into the lives of the people around me. And thank You for its boomerang effect! Amen.

DREAM BIG

May your day be fashioned with joy,
sprinkled with dreams, and touched by the miracle of love.

Allow your dreams a place in your prayers and plans. God-given dreams can help you move into the future He is preparing for you. A little girl once wrote on her science paper, "When you breathe, you *inspire*. When you do not breathe, you *expire*." Dreaming should be as natural as breathing. But who among us hasn't suffered from a broken dream or two? When that happens, we suffer a kind of spiritual death and need to surrender our lost dream to Christ, asking Him either to restore it or to give us a brand-new one.

Even daydreams can be gifts of God, so it's important to pay attention to them. Experts claim they can reveal things that help us organize our time, develop our goals, and cope with our problems. Taking a few moments to daydream can also calm, relax, and give you perspective.

The psalmists frequently focused on peaceful images. Psalm 23 speaks of quiet waters, a sumptuous table, and green pastures. Thinking about such a place must have quieted David's spirit and strengthened his faith. Even the image of the dark valley was redeemed by the image of God walking through it beside him. This kind of daydreaming renews. "He restoreth my soul," wrote David (Ps. 23:3 KJV).

Close your eyes right now and use every one of your senses to dwell on thoughts that bring you closer to God. You might start by reading the last chapter of Revelation, which is filled with amazing mental images of the great things God has in store for those who love Him. These are God's special dreams for His children.

As you dream, keep in mind these ABCs.

Aim high.
Believe in God.
Consider your options.
Don't give up.
Enrich your soul.
Find faith in doubt.
Go for the grace.
Hang on.
Ignore discouragement.
Just let Jesus!
Keep trying.
Love life.
Make merry.
Never say, "I can't."
Open your mind.
Pray hard.
Quit whining.
Read the Bible.
Stay strong.
Take on the challenge.
Understand the obstacles.

Value virtue.
Wait patiently.
X-ccelerate hope.
Yield to the Holy Spirit.
Zero in on joy.

Today pray over your dreams, asking for God's blessing and guidance. Then write them down in the form of goals and seal them in an envelope. Entrust it to a friend, asking that it be returned to you in one year. Meanwhile whenever these dreams cross your mind, think about them with faith and enthusiasm and commit them to the Lord. Take whatever steps He invites you to take, but don't worry about feverishly pursuing them, because this will only rob you of energy. Thank God for His way of making those dreams come true.

Still, there will be obstacles. When trouble assaults your dreams, think TICDAABGC—Things I Can't Do Anything About But God Can! Make a list of all these things and then post the list on your bathroom mirror. Add items as necessary. Now affirm your commitment to God's love, life, and laughter. Wake up each morning with faith on your lips and tuck yourself into bed each evening in faith's comforting blankets. God can take the sour, bitter things in your life and blend them into something that smells and tastes as sweet as honey. Generate enthusiasm wherever you go; it will power your dreams!

There are three kinds of people in this world: those who make things happen, those who watch things happen, and those who don't know what on earth is happening. Which kind will you be? Paul wrote, "Forgetting those things which are behind, and reaching forth unto those things which are before, I press toward the mark for the prize" (Phil. 3:13–14 KJV).

Don't you want to inspire others like that? I do. I will do my best with what I have as long as I am able. A student once wrote, "Dew is formed on leaves when the sun shines down on them and makes them perspire." The heat of life may make me sweat, but it is going to be given back to the world as shining dewdrops.

Ambition is sometimes a negative word, connoting overblown egos and ruthless self-promotion. But when ambition means dreaming God's big dreams for your life, it's another matter. Here's my prayer for you as you head for your dreams: May the Lord bless thee and keepeth thee going!

UPLIFTER

He who overcomes will inherit all this, and I will be his God and he will be my son.

REVELATION 21:7

WAY TO PRAY

Dear Lord, so many dreams, so little time! What am I to do? Guide me and lead me, even if it means only taking one small step after another. I will give You free reign in my life to do Your will, thankful I am Your child. Amen.

LIFE HAPPENS

Pity the people who have no opinion,
for they shall go through life without a bumper sticker.

If you've come through some tough spots, remember this little ditty.

The next time you're discouraged, feeling mighty blue;
Take a look at the mighty oak to see what a nut can do.

No matter how crazy or nutty your life has seemed, God can make something strong and good out of it. He can help you grow wide branches for others to shelter under.

A father wrote to me several years ago, saying,

It has been close to two years now since our college-age son told us he was gay. Guess what, Barb? We're still here! Even more, we're smiling and praising God. No, our son hasn't "gone straight," but we are experiencing God's peace.... There was no pill we took that made it better ... but by immersing ourselves in the love of those who shared and understood our hurt ... we received the assurance that we would survive! Another brick on the path to recovery was when we got past our introspection and attended to reaching out to others who were hurting. . . . We've moved from "Why me, Lord?" to "Thank You, Lord!"

That dad is celebrating the fact that God is in control and that He loves us no matter what we're going through. In His eyes we are special. One of the most cherished gifts I have received is a beautiful red plate with these words painted around the edges: "You Are Special Today." Among early American families, whenever someone deserved praise or attention, they were served dinner on a red plate. What a neat way to celebrate! I wish I'd had that plate about fifty years ago. When you come to visit me, you'll see it proudly displayed. It reminds me that even when it isn't anybody's birthday or any holiday at all, God loves us every day, filling us with His presence.

Why am I so special to the Lord? Because He sees me through the rich red blood of Jesus Christ. You too are somebody special, number one with God. Even so, our status as God's children doesn't mean life will be easy. Because He wants us to know true joy rather than just mere pleasure, God often digs wells of joy with the spade of sorrow. But the God who knows our load limit will graciously limit our load. Though He may not change our circumstances, He will certainly change us.

Each of us have three persons to contend with: the person I was, the person I am, and the person I will become. If you can forgive the person you were, accept the person you are, and believe in the person you will become, you are headed for joy. So celebrate *your* life. Get close to as many warm personalities as possible! Read God's Word, for a Bible that is falling apart probably belongs to someone whose life is not.

Many times parents whose kids have taken a detour from God's best ask me for words of comfort. I tell them we simply aren't given a final score while the game is still being played; in fact, it isn't even halftime yet. God never promised we'd be leading at the half, but He did tell us that we win in the end! Showing love even when a child is on a detour is the best course you can possibly steer when they are in trouble. The dad who wrote above added,

We stopped focusing on straightening out our child and acknowledged that was God's role. . . . Our son was able to let down his defenses and freely express his love toward us.

Jeremiah wrote that God has plans for us (29:11)! Flee temptation without leaving a forwarding address. Run to the outstretched arms of God. Sit down at His banquet. As Shannon, my daughter-in-love, says, let Him show you that wherever you are, that's where the party is! Life in God is a great big hug that lasts forever!

UPLIFTER

And we know that in all things God works for the good of those who love him.

ROMANS 8:28

WAY TO PRAY

Lord, thank You that I can depend on You to be with me and to guide me in the choices I need to make today. Amen.

MERRYMAKING

I'm not fifty—I'm eighteen with thirty-two years of experience!

This year many Americans will turn fifty. But fifty ain't what it used to be. Judith Jamison, artistic director and ballet choreographer, says, "What's nice about being fifty is the beat, the rhythm, the movement. Nobody's stopped." The tennis great Billie Jean King adds, "I think fifty now is what thirty-five used to be. Spiritually and emotionally you get stronger."

I never wrote a word until I was fifty years old. Now I have three million books in print in twenty-four languages, plus braille and large print. My publishers are as flabbergasted as I am, because I have never even attended a writing seminar. That just shows how God can use you even when you're living between estrogen and death. I like to remind myself that time is merely what keeps everything from happening at once. Have you heard about the seven stages of womanhood?

> In your twenties you want to wake up with romance.
> In your thirties you want to wake up married.
> At forty you want to wake up rich.
> At fifty, to wake up successful.
> At sixty, to wake up contented.

At seventy, to wake up healthy.
And at eighty you just want to wake up!

Smack-dab in the middle, the fifties are a time of meta-morphosis. When short hemlines came back into fashion, one woman dug a miniskirt out of a box at the back of her closet and tried it on. It looked great—except she couldn't figure out what to do with the other leg!

Some say that life is a test, that if it were the real thing, we would have received further instructions! But think again, because we have the Bible, the greatest instruction book of all! The Bible is a love story wherein God encourages us to make our lives meaningful. But more than 45 percent of all men, and 40 percent of women, say they are "still trying to figure out the meaning and purpose" of their lives. However, only 28 percent of women over age fifty say they are still trying to figure it out. So age on, girls—the best is yet to be! You know you're getting close to real maturity, by the way, when you are content to feel right about something without needing to prove another person wrong. Or as someone else said, when you progress from cock-sureness into thoughtful uncertainty.

A doctor recorded the complaints of some of his mid-life patients. One woman complained of feeling "lustless." Another woman requested a "monogram." He heard about "migrating" headaches and "mental-pause." But even menopause is not an ending but a pause—a time to regroup before making a fresh start. Gather your energy. Redefine your goals. Be glad for a change. Medical researchers say women get a surge of mental, spiritual, and physical energy after menopause. So get ready. Get set. Go! And remember that

each day is like a suitcase—every person gets the same size, but some people figure out how to pack more into theirs.

I always set aside the first day of every month to do something fun just for myself. Opening mail, cooking, and household chores are off-limits. Sometimes I try a new hairstyle or sit down in my favorite chair and go catalog shopping. Once I drove to a high bluff overlooking the freeway, parked, put on an inspirational music tape, and just watched all the activity below. The first of every month is my time to renew my soul.

Maybe your schedule doesn't allow you to take a whole day for yourself, but you can spend part of a day doing something fun: fly a kite, walk on the beach, pack a yummy lunch and find a special place to eat it. Enjoying yourself doesn't have to be expensive. You can do something I call "merry-making" anytime, anywhere. That's when you express your joy over small successes—like the time that awful stain came out of your dress, or your checkbook actually balanced.

Life is short. Each year passes more quickly than the previous one. It's easy to deny yourself many of life's simple pleasures because you want to be practical. Forget about practical and decide instead to become a joy collector. Always be on the lookout for gifts without ribbons. God is strewing them across your path right now. His gifts come tagged with a note: "Life can be wonderful. Do your best not to miss it!" Enjoy what is before it isn't anymore.

God will scatter surprise blessings across your path in the next few years. Don't be like the woman who described herself as passive and bored, a "mush melon living in a middle-aged frame." Instead be zany and giddy. Dare to slip on a pair of bunny slippers once in a while! Surprise yourself! Enjoy the little things because one day you'll look back and realize they were the big things!

UPLIFTER

For the kingdom of God is not a matter of eating and drinking, but of righteousness, peace and joy in the Holy Spirit. . . . Let us therefore make every effort to do what leads to peace and to mutual edification.
ROMANS 14:17, 19

WAY TO PRAY

Dear God, You help me see I don't need to get stuck in a mid-life crisis. Instead I want to step enthusiastically into Your kingdom life. No more blahs, bummies, or battles with gloom. I am waking up to Your great world, great people, and a great future. Thank You for rolling out the red carpet as I turn fifty. Amen!

BLESSED BY STRESS

Somewhere over the rainbow—
that's where the airline will find my luggage.

I'm not kidding. Even stress can be a blessing if you know how to deal with it. I first entered "the school of stress" during my teenage years when I attended a private Christian high school in the Deep South. As soon as I arrived, I saw a large sign: "Griping not tolerated." (Hmmm. In my family *griping* meant throwing up! I figured I could try not to throw up while I was at school.) Then I saw signs over the doors of every room in the school, signs like: "Do right" and "Don't sacrifice the permanent on the altar of the immediate." You get the idea. This school was very big on The Rules.

How could I possibly live according to all these rules every day? I thought it might just kill me. But it didn't. Instead of bucking the system, I did everything I could to cooperate. I learned then that there is a whole new way to react to things you do not like. When you go through a whole semester telling yourself, *I will not gripe,* not griping not only becomes a positive habit, it elevates your attitude.

Of course, it was exhausting trying to be so good all the time. But eventually I discovered that the real trick to dealing with stress is to kick it out of gear, roll with the punches, and take one day at a time. Instead of asking God to get rid of it, I had to learn to neutralize its effect. I discovered that winners turn stress into something good, while losers let stress turn life into something bad. Winners see an answer for every problem, while losers see a problem for every answer. Knowing these differences and incorporating them into the way you face stress is key to keeping your dignity and peace in adversity.

Some people just can't seem to get the hang of it. A friend wrote, "Barbara, I tried relaxing, but somehow I feel more comfortable being tense." Changing our patterned responses to life can be uncomfortable but well worth it.

A woman named Anna Mary Robertson refused to resign herself to the stress of aging. After rearing ten children and despite being plagued with arthritis in her hands, she took up painting. Twenty-five percent of her work was completed after she had turned one hundred years old! We know her as Grandma Moses, the gifted artist who produced more than fifteen hundred sought after paintings.

Another elderly woman modeled stress reduction based on her love of the Bible, especially Psalm 91:4, which reads, "He will cover you with his feathers." Whenever this lady experienced stress, she would repeat to herself, "I am covered with feathers. I am covered with feathers." One night while walking down a dark street, she realized she was being followed by two men. Fearful, she began to affirm out loud, "I am covered with feathers! I am covered with feathers!"

One of the would-be muggers shouted, "Hey, man, this lady is crazy. Let's get out of here!" And they fled!

Emily Dickinson wrote, "Hope is the thing with feathers that perches in the soul." It's a wonder Paul didn't include feathers in the armor of God, described in the book of Ephesians. Paul tells us we need to be fully clothed in order to fend off the fiery darts of our Enemy. Yet too many of us are like Christian streakers. We put on the helmet of salvation but forget about the rest of our armor. To beat stress, we also need the belt of truth, the breastplate of righteousness, the shoes of readiness to share God's peace, and the shield of faith. Oh, and let's not forget about the feathers!

The truth is that every day has its share of stress. When you feel like an aerosol can because you are under too much pressure, find a listening ear to act as a safety valve. Throw a pity party for your friends so you can all get it out of your system at once. Drown your fears in compassion for each other and then rise up and give yourselves a great big hug. Encourage each other to hang on and hang in there! As Launa Herrmann says, "If you keep hanging in there, your wrists won't stretch, but your adaptability will!"

I've come to believe that big crosses—every once in a while—work to our advantage, for they teach us to bear the little ones calmly. What about tomorrow? Let God worry about it! It belongs to Him.

UPLIFTER

A righteous man may have many troubles, but the LORD delivers him from them all.

PSALM 34:19

WAY TO PRAY

Lord, I don't want to corner the market on stress. I am doing the best I can to let it go. I pray for light and love along the path, enough to see me through. I know You are there for me every step of the way. Amen.

KEEP AT IT!

Noah didn't wait for his ship to come in—he built it himself!

I'm always fascinated by the life stories of entrepreneurs, athletes, musicians, and others who've made it to the top. How on earth do they endure the grueling training, intense discipline, and moments of devastating failure along their way up? With hindsight it's easy to see that all their efforts were worth it. But en route they must have wondered. They must have battled the same self-doubts and insecurities we all do.

Figure skater Scott Hamilton, back on the ice after recovering from chemotherapy, says with a broad smile, "You have to see that you are the driving force in your own life!" Someone else expressed it this way: "The Lord gave us two ends—one to sit on and the other to think with. Success depends on which one we use the most!"

Inspiring stories help us believe that we too can overcome obstacles and achieve great things. We are responsible for nurturing our faith in God, in ourselves, in our dreams. It's up to us to keep trying and keep believing. But there is more. We are also responsible for helping others on their trek up the mountain. Every day, we meet people who could use a boost of encouragement just to keep going.

A group of students from the Philippines traveled to the Precious Moments Chapel in Carthage, Missouri, to see Sam Butcher, the man who had for so many years supported the Bible college they attended. They also wanted to see the artwork that had been his gift to the Lord. One evening the students presented a musical program prepared just for Sam. A young pianist played so beautifully, it touched him deeply. When Sam complimented him, the young man surprised him by reminding him, "But Mr. Butcher, it is because of you I play. When I was only six years old in the Philippines, you gave me a piano and said, 'The Lord has given you a special gift. If you use it for Him, He will bless you.' You were right! I travel all over and am often told how my music is a blessing!"

Even small gifts can carry tremendous boomerang power. A wink, a smile, a note of appreciation, or a bouquet given in love—all these can inspire others to use their gifts.

Sam Butcher's kindness boomeranged again one day as he worked hard putting the finishing touches on the ceiling and walls at the Precious Moments Chapel. As he was leaving for the day, he saw the security guards at the gates explaining to a pair of would-be visitors that the Chapel was not yet open. But instead of turning the couple away, Sam invited them to be his personal guests to tour the Chapel. They loved what they saw and asked if their son might come and see the Chapel, too, even though it wasn't finished.

"No problem," Sam said. "Just have him give me a call."

A few days later Sam received a call from the couple's son. On the other end of the line was John Ashcroft, the governor of the state of Missouri, who later agreed to be the speaker at the opening and dedication of the Chapel!

You never know how a humble gesture of hospitality might boomerang back. The key is not success but kindness. Success simply gives you a broader platform from which you may look for opportunities to do good, to respect others, and to show love. Whether bringing your own goals into focus or helping someone else achieve theirs, keep at it. Do better than you did yesterday. Work hard. Determine to do what you can do. Go the second mile. You just might stumble on a treasure while you're at it. Faith can move mountains, but only hard work can dig a tunnel through them!

UPLIFTER

Keep on loving each other as brothers. Do not forget to entertain strangers, for by so doing some people have entertained angels without knowing it.

HEBREWS 13:1–2

WAY TO PRAY

Loving Father and almighty God, how precious are Your thoughts toward me. You are always looking out for me, always on my side. May I be like You, showing other people that I care, that I am on their side. Together the bunch of us make such a great team! Amen.

DRAW A CONCLUSION

A conclusion is simply the place
where you land when you get tired of thinking.

When Bill and I started Spatula Ministries many years ago, we worked with hurting parents coping with losing a child either through death or through the homosexual lifestyle. Now we're deluged with letters from parents who are grappling with several tragedies simultaneously. These mothers and fathers are basically saying, "We've walked through the fire (that aroma we wear is actually the smoky scent of lingering disaster)."

I always answer, "The truth will set you free, but first it will make you miserable."

I also try to assure them that their lives will eventually be enriched by experiences they endure with grace. We produce fruit by the calamities that fertilize our lives.

The truth is that even in the midst of trouble, happy moments swim by us every day, like shining, silver fish waiting to be caught. For every one thing that goes wrong, I've concluded, a hundred blessings arise out of it. The next time you find yourself caught in a web of unanswerable "why's," imagine your problems as a convoluted mass of yarn with tangles you could never straighten out. Then imagine yourself dropping these tangles into God's hands, knowing He alone can untangle the threads, weaving them together into a pattern that makes sense. Speaking of threads, there is a Christian singing group who calls one of their tours *Threads*. I like that name. Their point is that we are all threads, some new and shining, others worn, ragged, and to the point of breaking. Still, we all belong together on the loom of life. Only together do we make the pattern God has in mind. We need each other.

I need you, you need me, and our sister over there needs both of us. One mother wrote that her holidays were always miserable because she was estranged from her only child. The next Mother's Day she sent cards to all the new mothers she knew and to her friends who were mothers. She accepted a dinner invitation and took lilacs and candy to her hostess, a lady in her eighties. She used every holiday from then on to bring joy to others lonelier than herself.

Dr. Karl Menninger, the world-famous psychiatrist, was once answering questions after giving a lecture on mental health. Someone asked, "What would you advise a person to do if he felt a nervous breakdown coming on?" Most people expected Menninger to say, "Consult a psychiatrist." Instead he said, "Lock up your house, go across the railroad tracks, find someone in need, and do something to help that person." Dr. Menninger knew that the only difference between a stumbling block and a stepping-stone is the way you use it!

A Christian woman saw a homeless girl out in the cold, shivering in a thin dress. She looked weak and limp from hunger. The woman prayed, "Dear God, why don't You do something to help that little girl and others like her?"

God replied, "I already did—I made you!"

Use your hindsight to improve your foresight. Whatever happens, start with prayer and then take a step further. By now you will have drawn the conclusion that boomerang joy will bring healing to your life and the lives of many, many others. Fling it out! Shout it out! And watch it come right back to you.

FLING IT OUT!

When someone does a kindness
That brightens up your day,
When a good friend helps you smile although
Your heart's chock-full of pain . . .
When a gift comes unexpectedly
To make your spirits rise,
When a little word is said
To put a twinkle in your eye . . .
Don't forget to fling that kindness
Right back out to someone else.
Send it on with sweet abandon—
Don't just keep it for yourself.
For joy that's shared is a boomerang.
Each kindness that you do,
Each smile you share, each heart you lift
Flings joy right back to you.

249

UPLIFTER

Now is your time of grief, but I will see you again and you will rejoice, and no one will take away your joy.

JOHN 16:22

WAY TO PRAY

Lord, what I am going through right now isn't the end of my story. Every tomorrow is still in Your hand. My next moment, the very next breath I draw, is a gift from You. I offer You my burdens and say, "Whatever, Lord." I rest now, relieved that You have joy ahead for me. Full, overflowing joy. Amen.

We want to hear from you. Please send your comments
about this book to us in care of the address below.
Thank you.

ZondervanPublishingHouse
Grand Rapids, Michigan 49530
http://www.zondervan.com